TABLE OF CONTENTS

The Birth of an Explorer

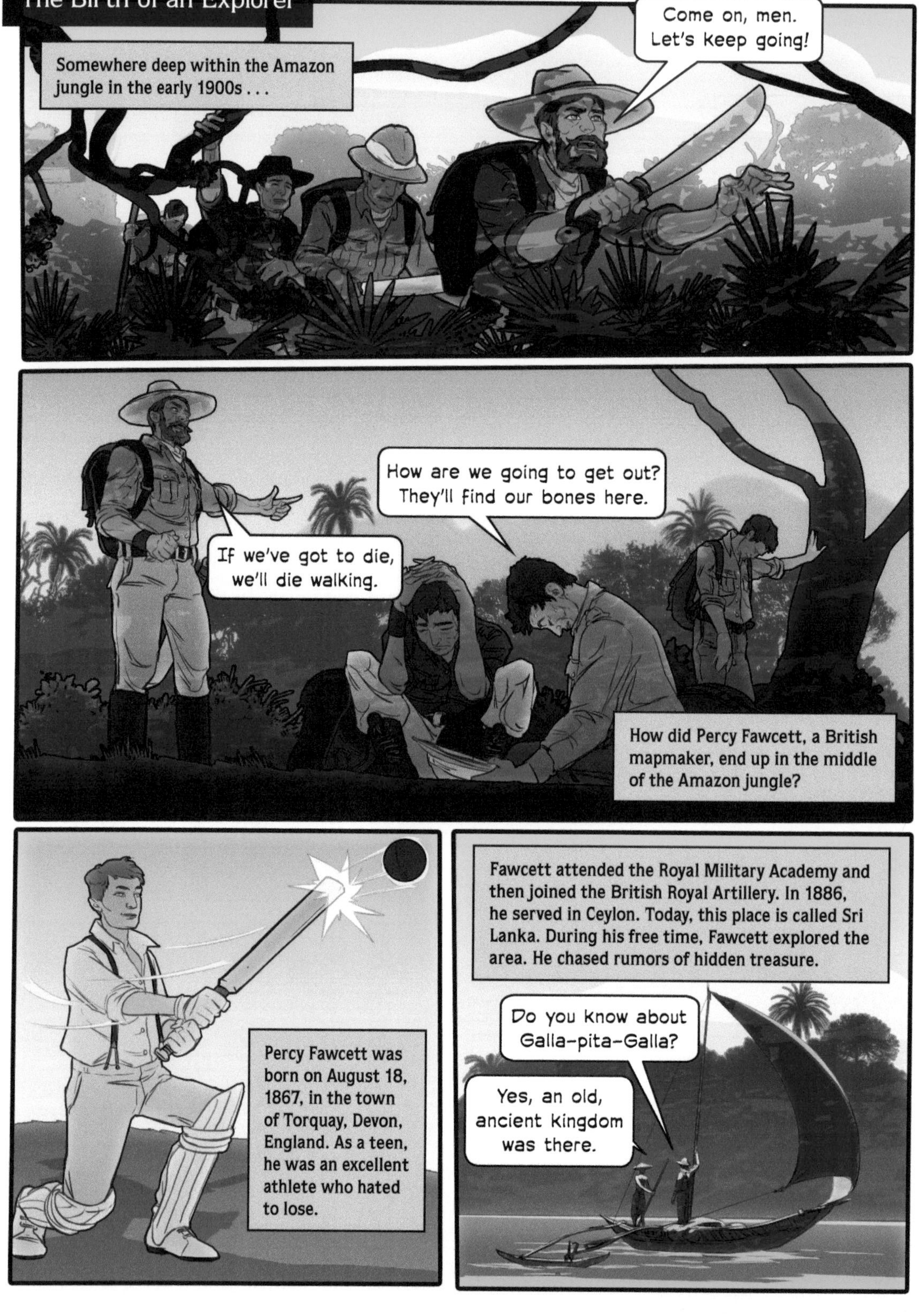

Somewhere deep within the Amazon jungle in the early 1900s . . .
Come on, men. Let's keep going!
If we've got to die, we'll die walking.
How are we going to get out? They'll find our bones here.
How did Percy Fawcett, a British mapmaker, end up in the middle of the Amazon jungle?
Percy Fawcett was born on August 18, 1867, in the town of Torquay, Devon, England. As a teen, he was an excellent athlete who hated to lose.
Fawcett attended the Royal Military Academy and then joined the British Royal Artillery. In 1886, he served in Ceylon. Today, this place is called Sri Lanka. During his free time, Fawcett explored the area. He chased rumors of hidden treasure.
Do you know about Galla-pita-Galla?
Yes, an old, ancient kingdom was there.

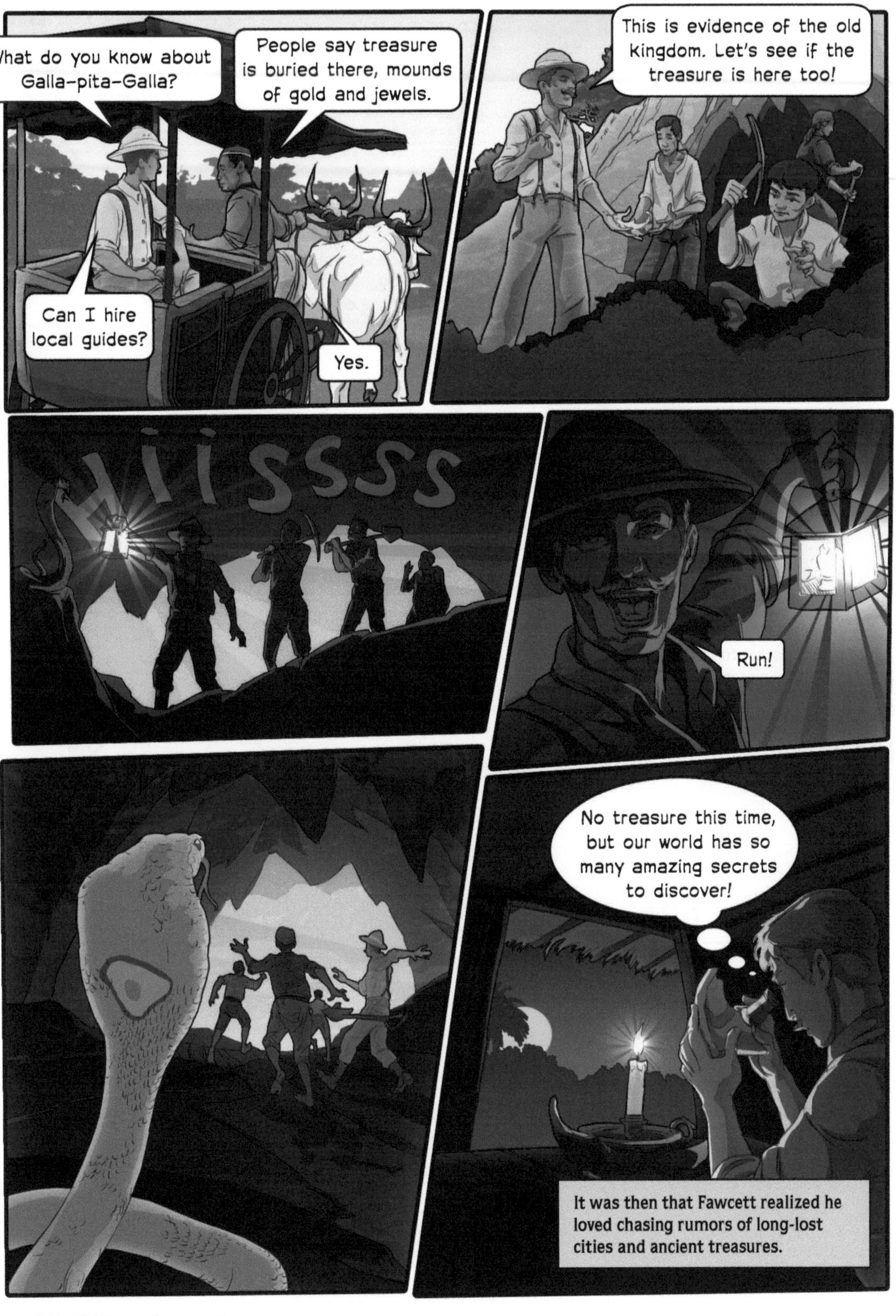
What do you know about Galla-pita-Galla?
People say treasure is buried there, mounds of gold and jewels.
Can I hire local guides?
Yes.
This is evidence of the old kingdom. Let's see if the treasure is here too!
HISSSS
Run!
No treasure this time, but our world has so many amazing secrets to discover!
It was then that Fawcett realized he loved chasing rumors of long-lost cities and ancient treasures.

Fawcett's First Expeditions

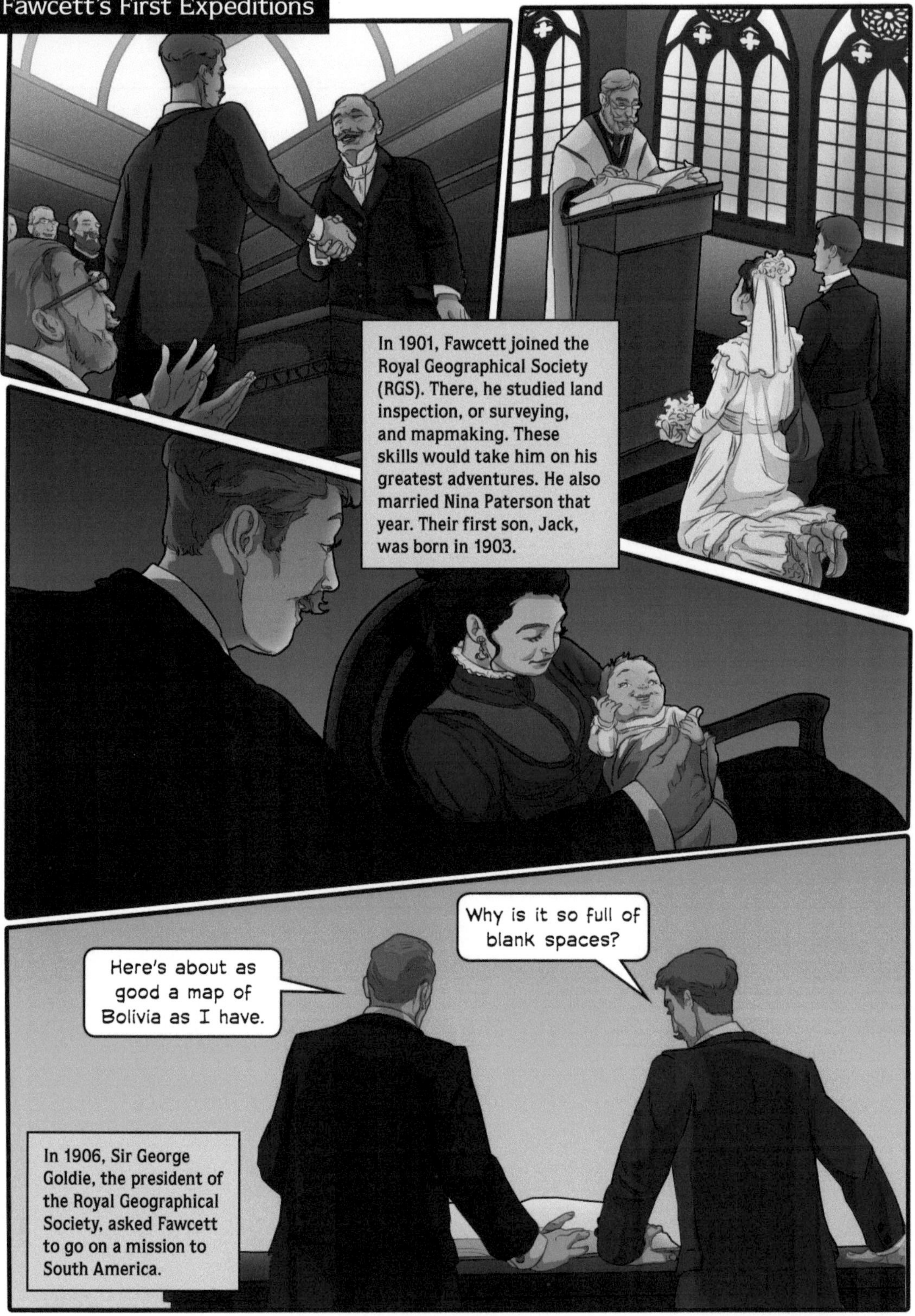
In 1901, Fawcett joined the Royal Geographical Society (RGS). There, he studied land inspection, or surveying, and mapmaking. These skills would take him on his greatest adventures. He also married Nina Paterson that year. Their first son, Jack, was born in 1903.
In 1906, Sir George Goldie, the president of the Royal Geographical Society, asked Fawcett to go on a mission to South America.
Here's about as good a map of Bolivia as I have.
Why is it so full of blank spaces?

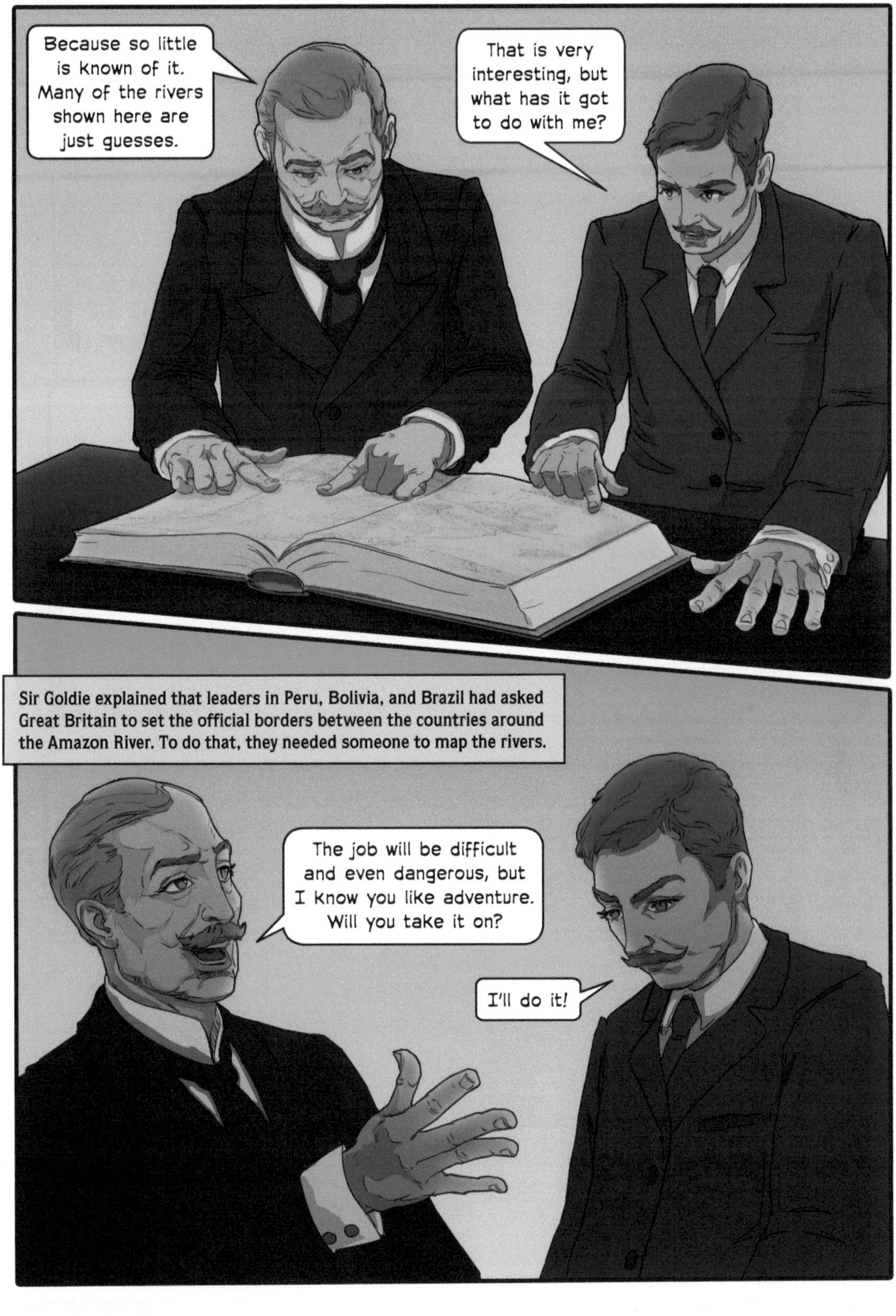
Because so little is known of it. Many of the rivers shown here are just guesses.
That is very interesting, but what has it got to do with me?
Sir Goldie explained that leaders in Peru, Bolivia, and Brazil had asked Great Britain to set the official borders between the countries around the Amazon River. To do that, they needed someone to map the rivers.
The job will be difficult and even dangerous, but I know you like adventure. Will you take it on?
I'll do it!

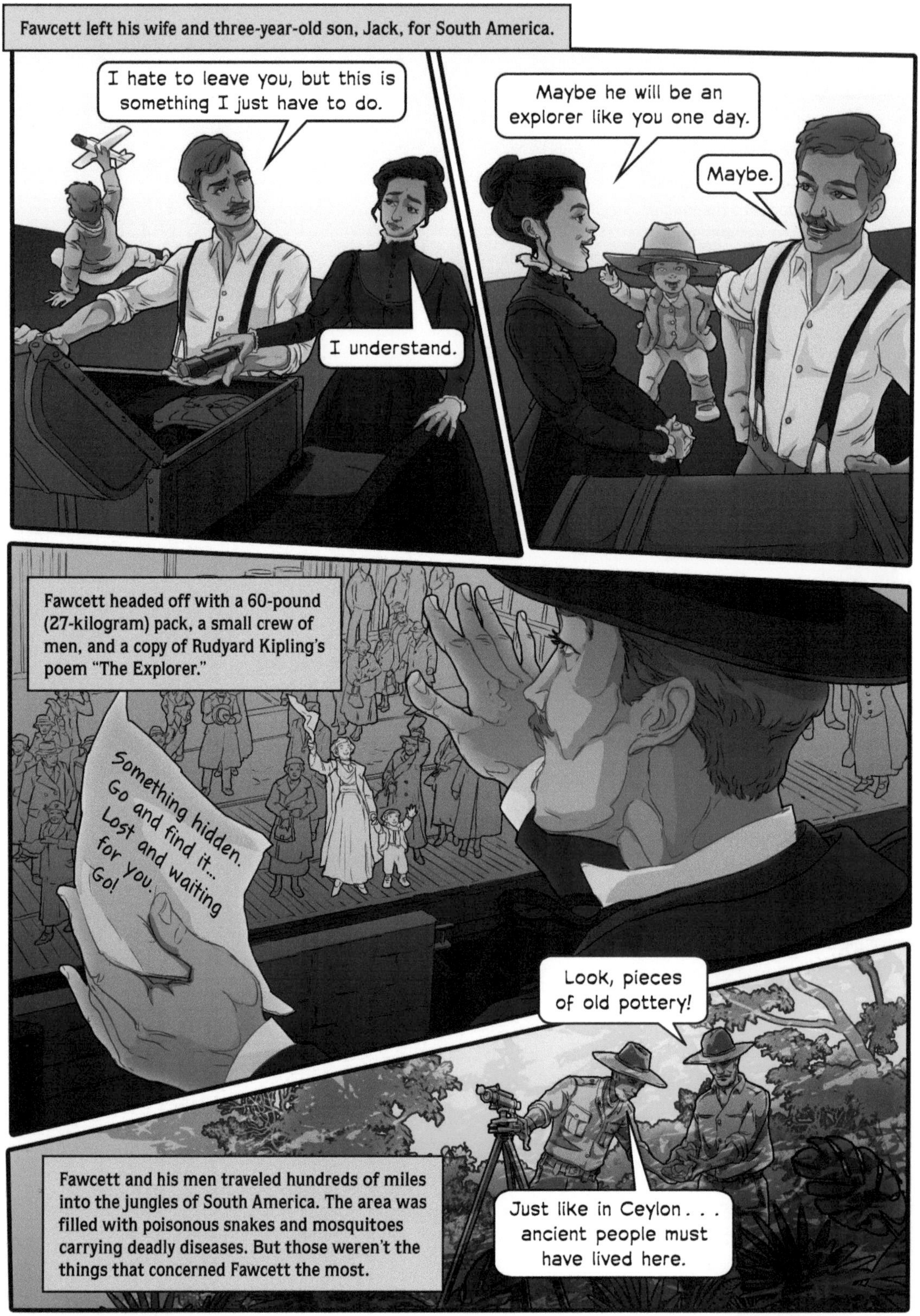
Fawcett left his wife and three-year-old son, Jack, for South America.
I hate to leave you, but this is something I just have to do.
I understand.
Maybe he will be an explorer like you one day.
Maybe.
Fawcett headed off with a 60-pound (27-kilogram) pack, a small crew of men, and a copy of Rudyard Kipling's poem "The Explorer."
Something hidden. Go and find it... Lost and waiting for you. Go!
Look, pieces of old pottery!
Fawcett and his men traveled hundreds of miles into the jungles of South America. The area was filled with poisonous snakes and mosquitoes carrying deadly diseases. But those weren't the things that concerned Fawcett the most.
Just like in Ceylon . . . ancient people must have lived here.

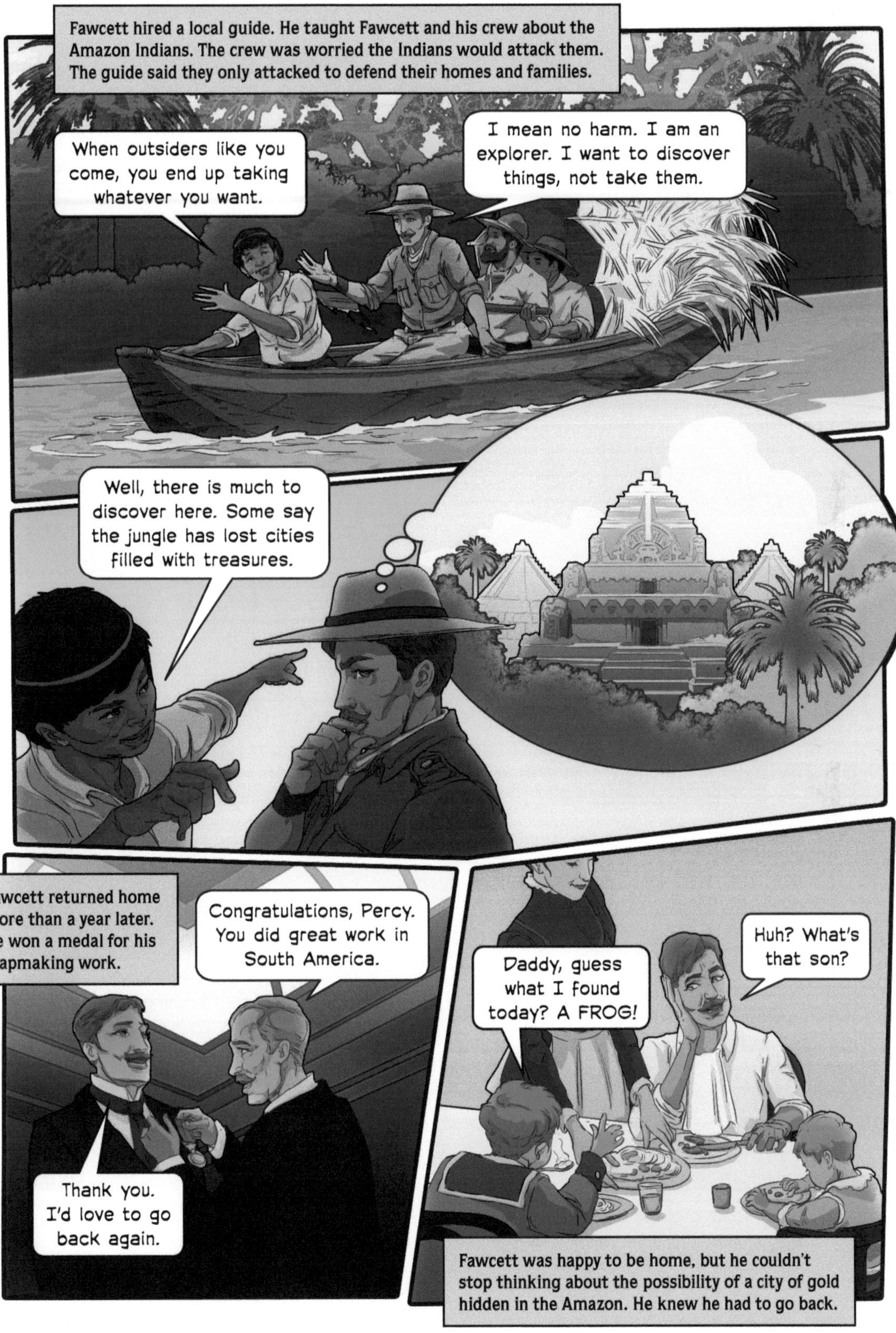
Fawcett hired a local guide. He taught Fawcett and his crew about the Amazon Indians. The crew was worried the Indians would attack them. The guide said they only attacked to defend their homes and families.
When outsiders like you come, you end up taking whatever you want.
I mean no harm. I am an explorer. I want to discover things, not take them.
Well, there is much to discover here. Some say the jungle has lost cities filled with treasures.
Fawcett returned home more than a year later. He won a medal for his mapmaking work.
Congratulations, Percy. You did great work in South America.
Thank you. I'd love to go back again.
Daddy, guess what I found today? A FROG!
Huh? What's that son?
Fawcett was happy to be home, but he couldn't stop thinking about the possibility of a city of gold hidden in the Amazon. He knew he had to go back.

Returning to the Amazon Again and Again

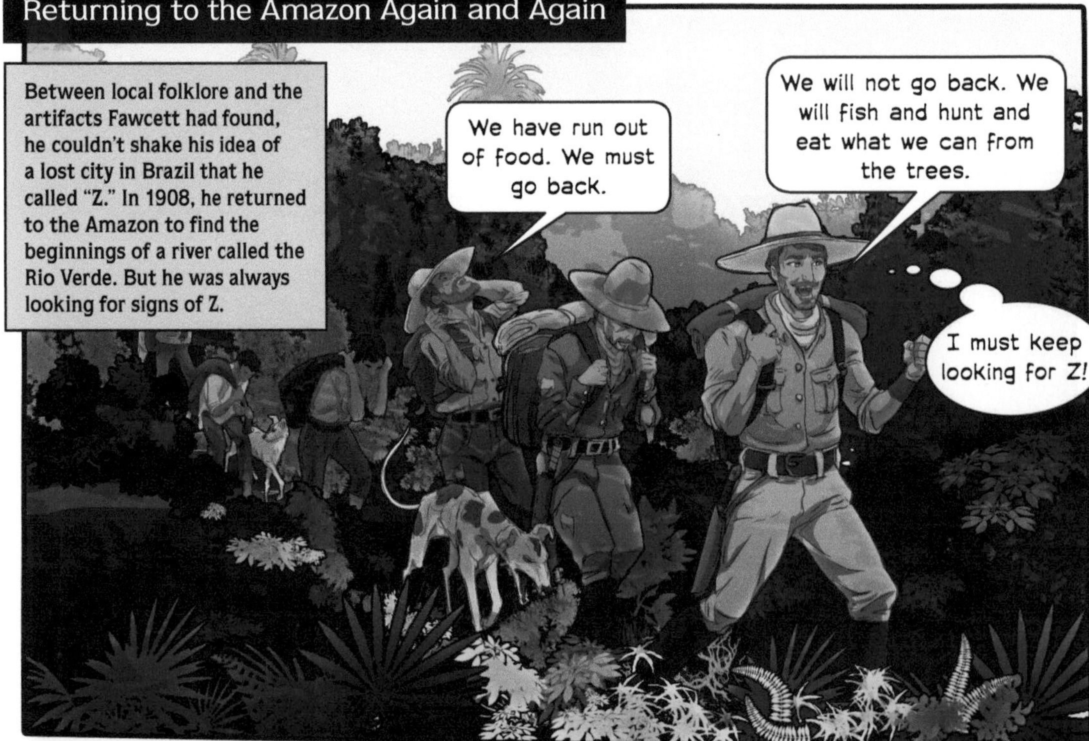
Between local folklore and the artifacts Fawcett had found, he couldn't shake his idea of a lost city in Brazil that he called "Z." In 1908, he returned to the Amazon to find the beginnings of a river called the Rio Verde. But he was always looking for signs of Z.
We have run out of food. We must go back.
We will not go back. We will fish and hunt and eat what we can from the trees.
I must keep looking for Z!

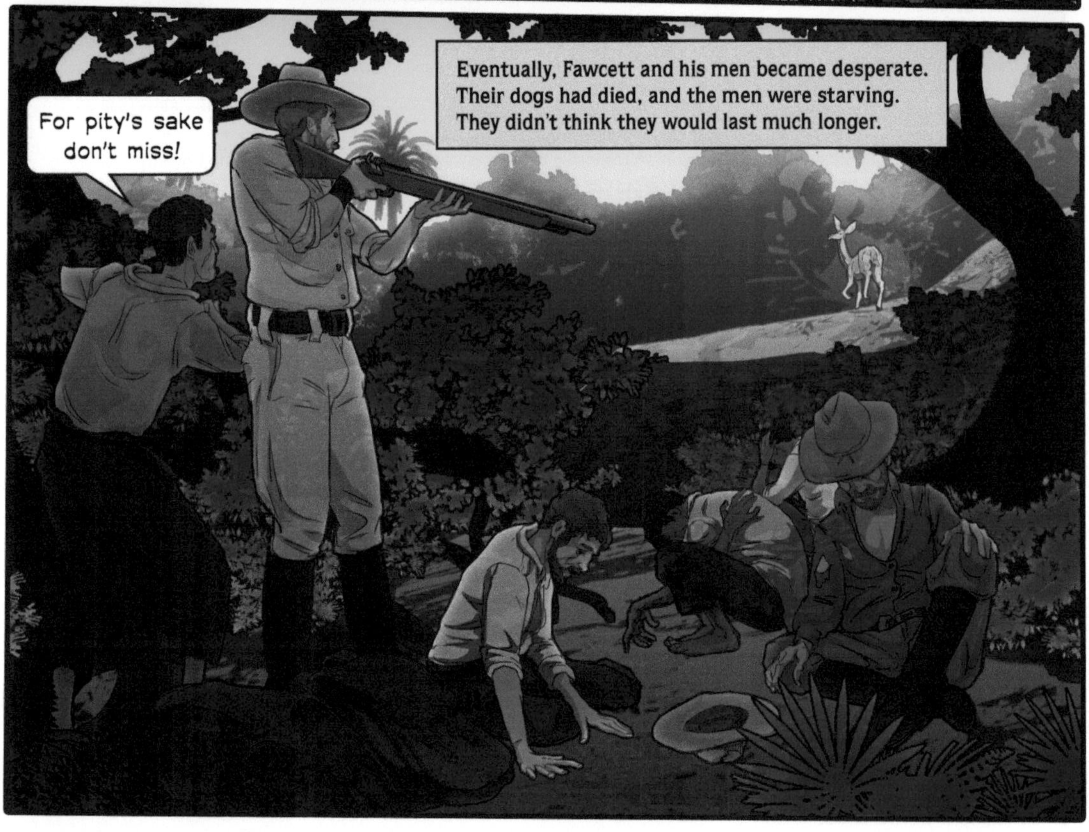
For pity's sake don't miss!
Eventually, Fawcett and his men became desperate. Their dogs had died, and the men were starving. They didn't think they would last much longer.

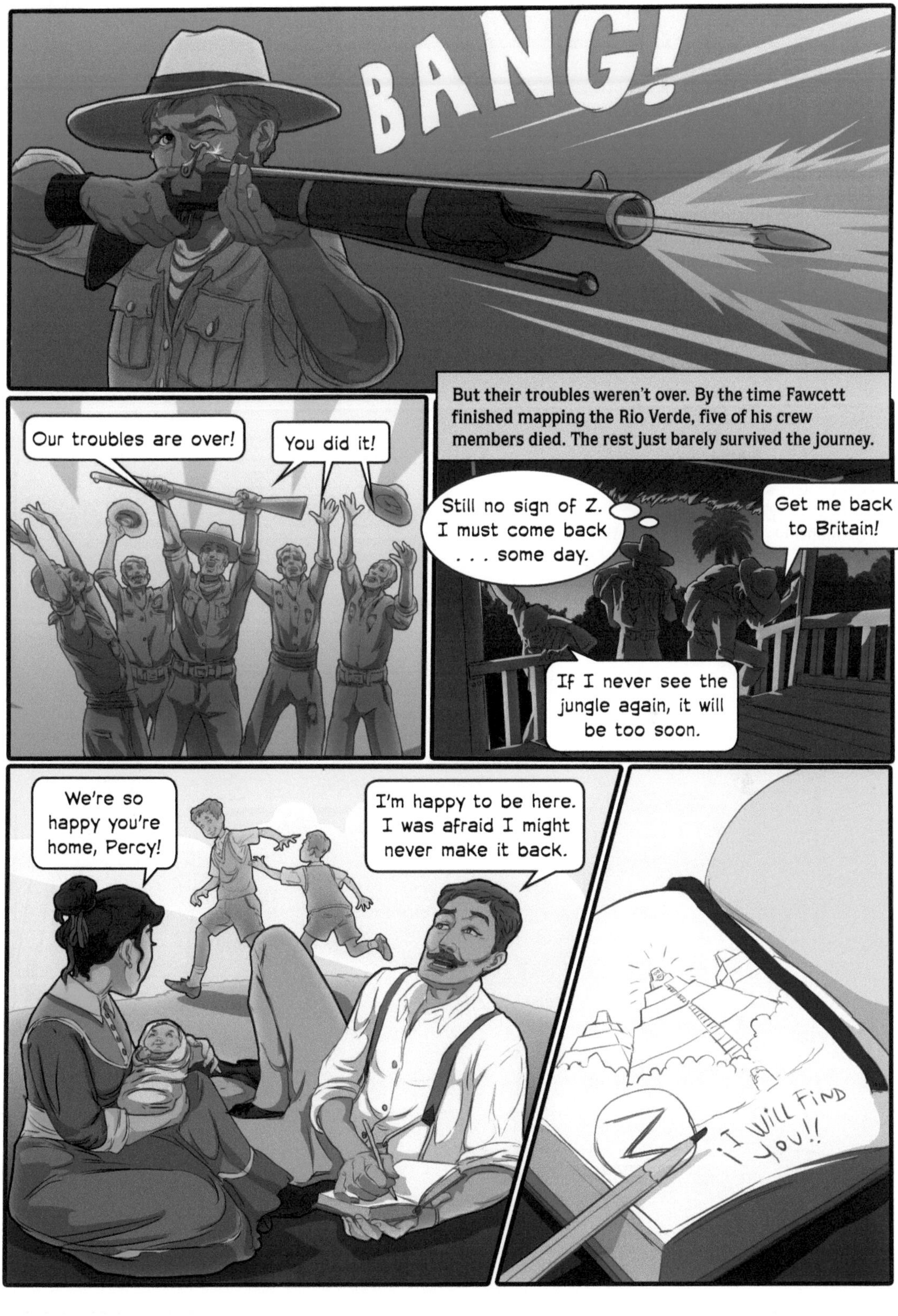
BANG!
But their troubles weren't over. By the time Fawcett finished mapping the Rio Verde, five of his crew members died. The rest just barely survived the journey.
Our troubles are over!
You did it!
Still no sign of Z. I must come back . . . some day.
Get me back to Britain!
If I never see the jungle again, it will be too soon.
We're so happy you're home, Percy!
I'm happy to be here. I was afraid I might never make it back.
Z
¡I WILL FIND YOU!!

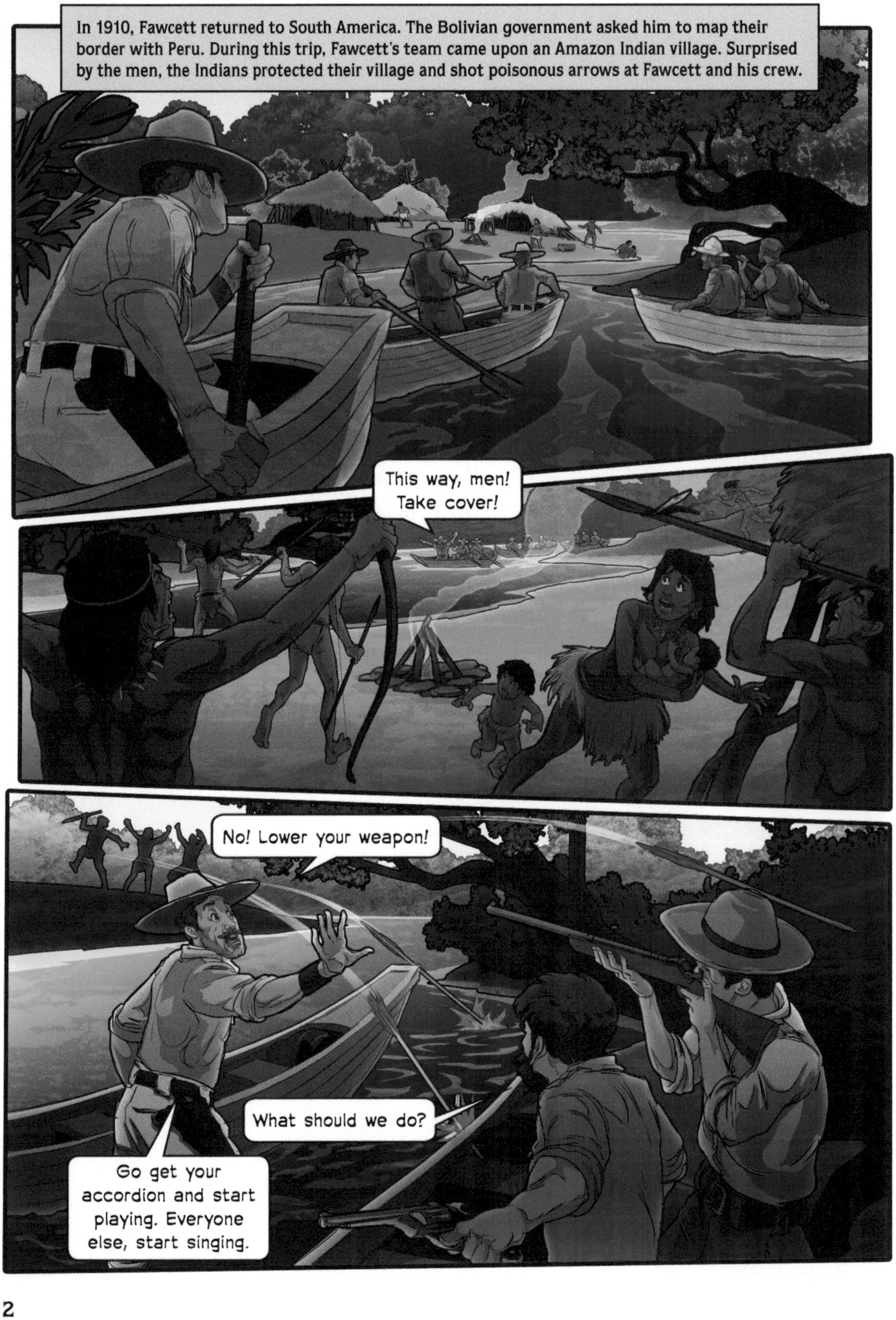
In 1910, Fawcett returned to South America. The Bolivian government asked him to map their border with Peru. During this trip, Fawcett's team came upon an Amazon Indian village. Surprised by the men, the Indians protected their village and shot poisonous arrows at Fawcett and his crew.
This way, men! Take cover!
No! Lower your weapon!
What should we do?
Go get your accordion and start playing. Everyone else, start singing.

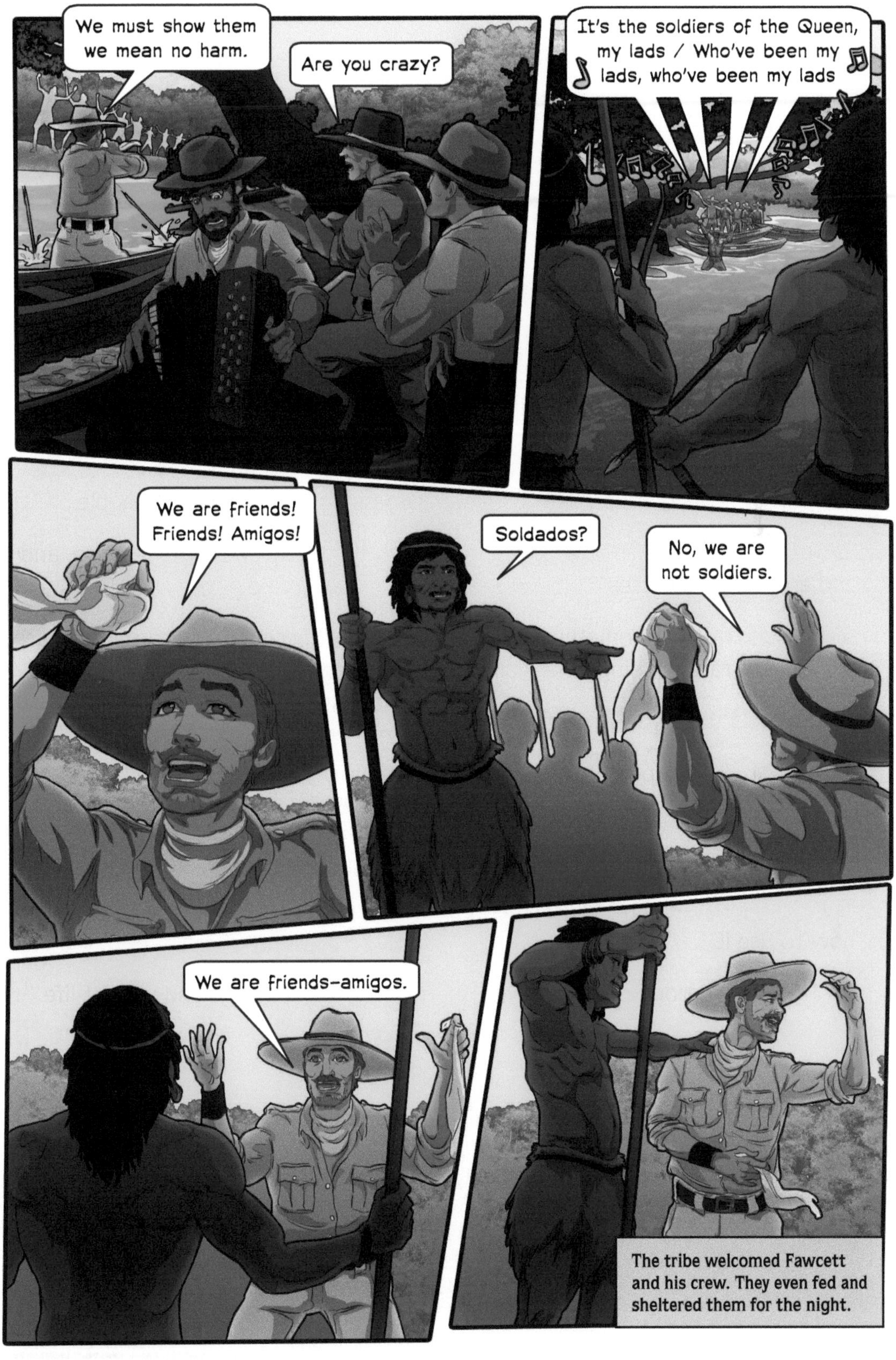
We must show them we mean no harm.
Are you crazy?
It's the soldiers of the Queen, my lads / Who've been my lads, who've been my lads
We are friends! Friends! Amigos!
Soldados?
No, we are not soldiers.
We are friends–amigos.
The tribe welcomed Fawcett and his crew. They even fed and sheltered them for the night.

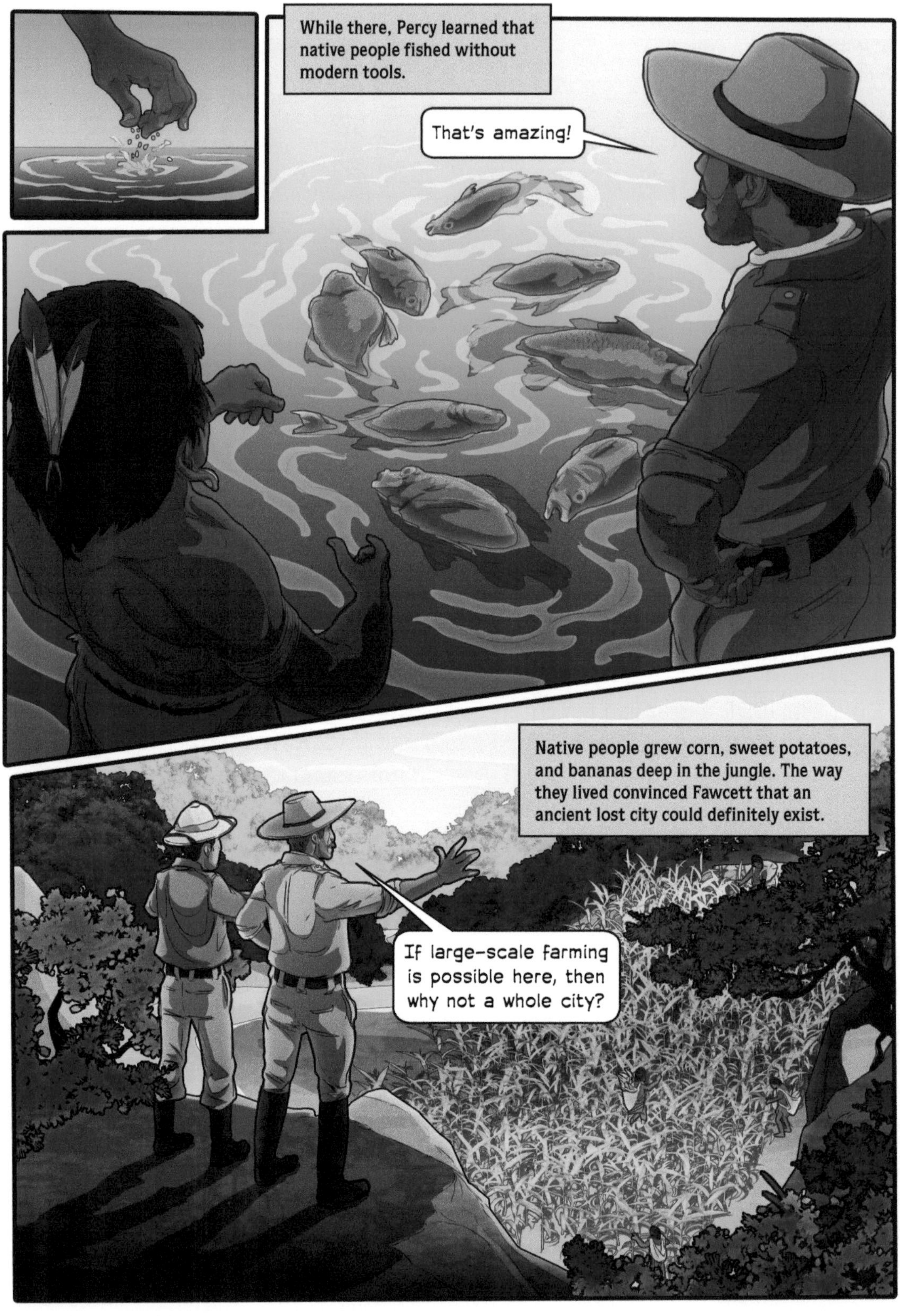
While there, Percy learned that native people fished without modern tools.
That's amazing!
Native people grew corn, sweet potatoes, and bananas deep in the jungle. The way they lived convinced Fawcett that an ancient lost city could definitely exist.
If large-scale farming is possible here, then why not a whole city?

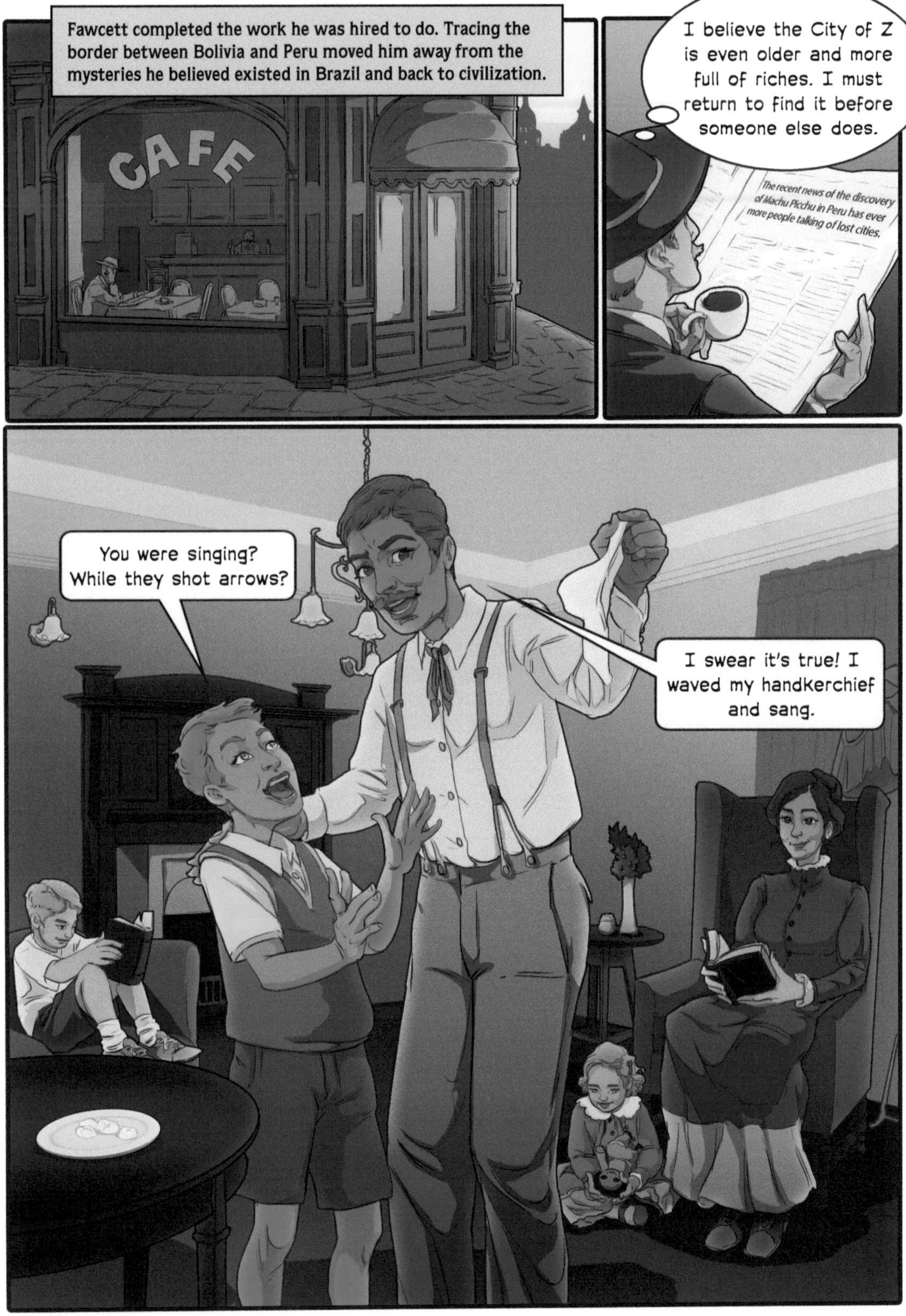
Fawcett completed the work he was hired to do. Tracing the border between Bolivia and Peru moved him away from the mysteries he believed existed in Brazil and back to civilization.
CAFE
I believe the City of Z is even older and more full of riches. I must return to find it before someone else does.
The recent news of the discovery of Machu Picchu in Peru has ever more people talking of lost cities.
You were singing? While they shot arrows?
I swear it's true! I waved my handkerchief and sang.

One Final Journey

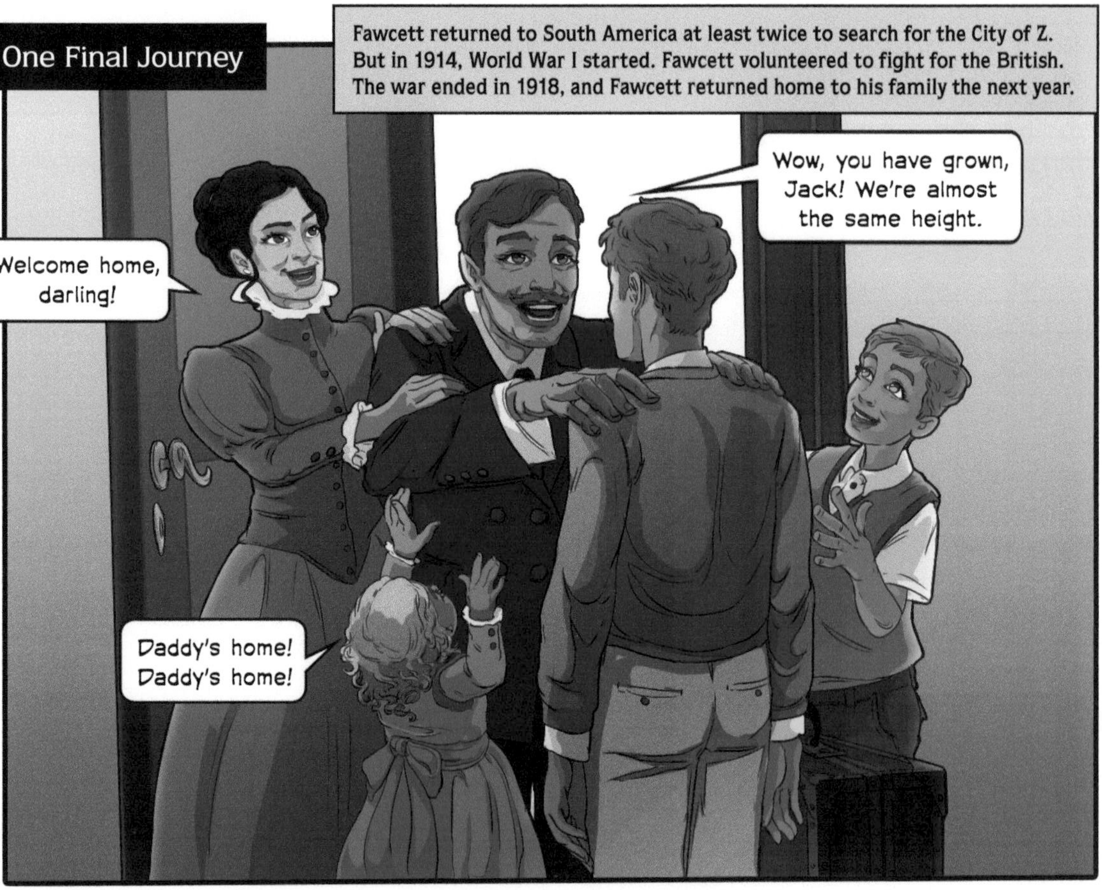
Fawcett returned to South America at least twice to search for the City of Z. But in 1914, World War I started. Fawcett volunteered to fight for the British. The war ended in 1918, and Fawcett returned home to his family the next year.
Welcome home, darling!
Wow, you have grown, Jack! We're almost the same height.
Daddy's home! Daddy's home!

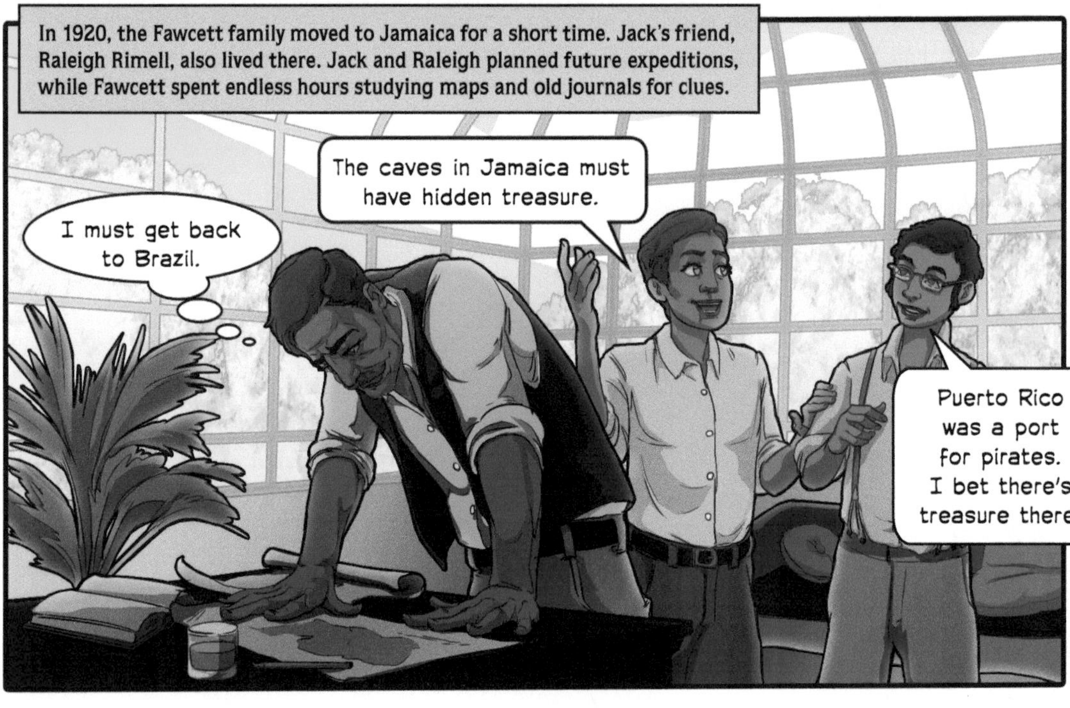
In 1920, the Fawcett family moved to Jamaica for a short time. Jack's friend, Raleigh Rimell, also lived there. Jack and Raleigh planned future expeditions, while Fawcett spent endless hours studying maps and old journals for clues.
I must get back to Brazil.
The caves in Jamaica must have hidden treasure.
Puerto Rico was a port for pirates. I bet there's treasure there.

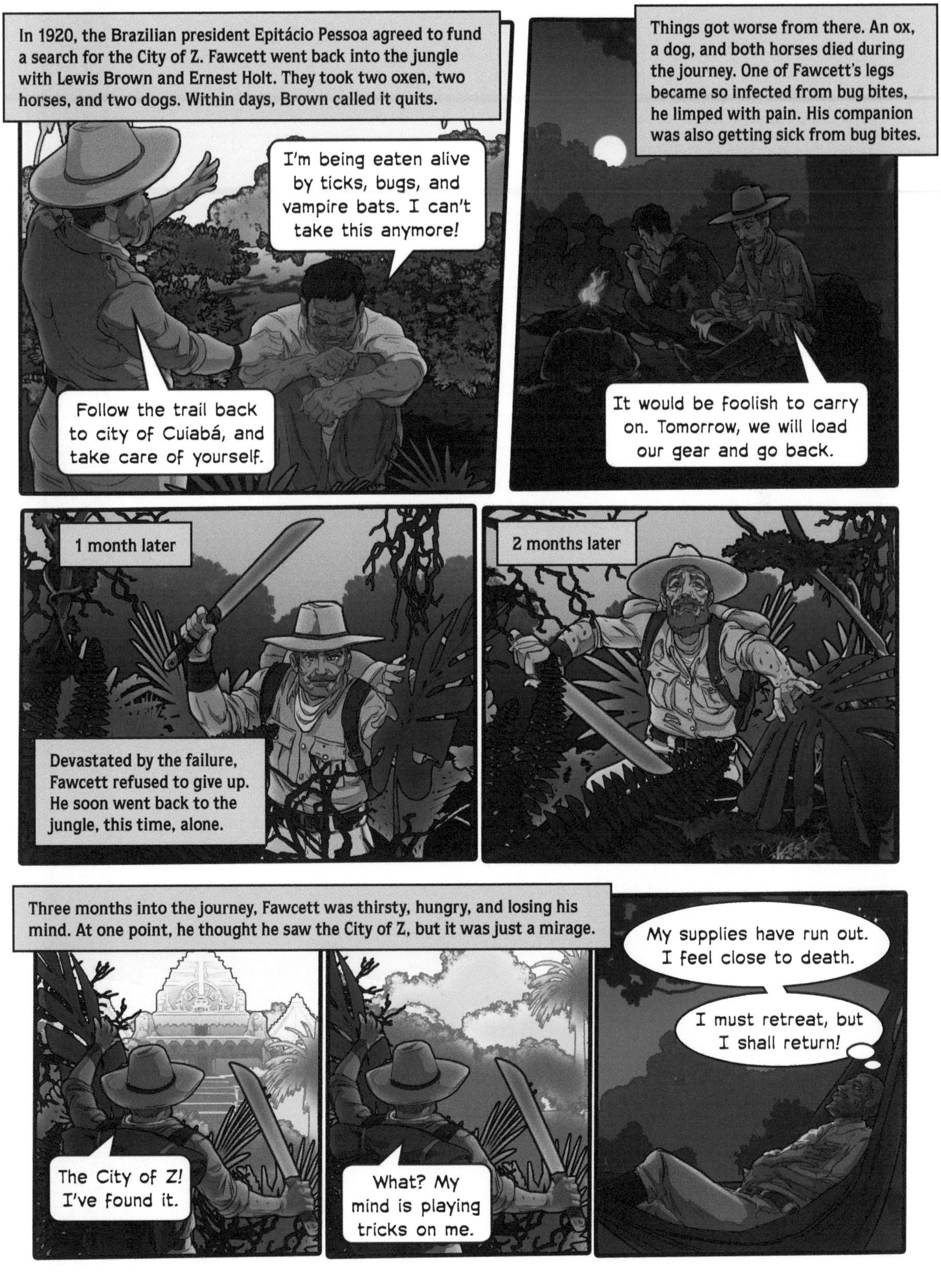
In 1920, the Brazilian president Epitácio Pessoa agreed to fund a search for the City of Z. Fawcett went back into the jungle with Lewis Brown and Ernest Holt. They took two oxen, two horses, and two dogs. Within days, Brown called it quits.
I'm being eaten alive by ticks, bugs, and vampire bats. I can't take this anymore!
Follow the trail back to city of Cuiabá, and take care of yourself.
Things got worse from there. An ox, a dog, and both horses died during the journey. One of Fawcett's legs became so infected from bug bites, he limped with pain. His companion was also getting sick from bug bites.
It would be foolish to carry on. Tomorrow, we will load our gear and go back.
1 month later
Devastated by the failure, Fawcett refused to give up. He soon went back to the jungle, this time, alone.
2 months later
Three months into the journey, Fawcett was thirsty, hungry, and losing his mind. At one point, he thought he saw the City of Z, but it was just a mirage.
The City of Z! I've found it.
What? My mind is playing tricks on me.
My supplies have run out. I feel close to death.
I must retreat, but I shall return!

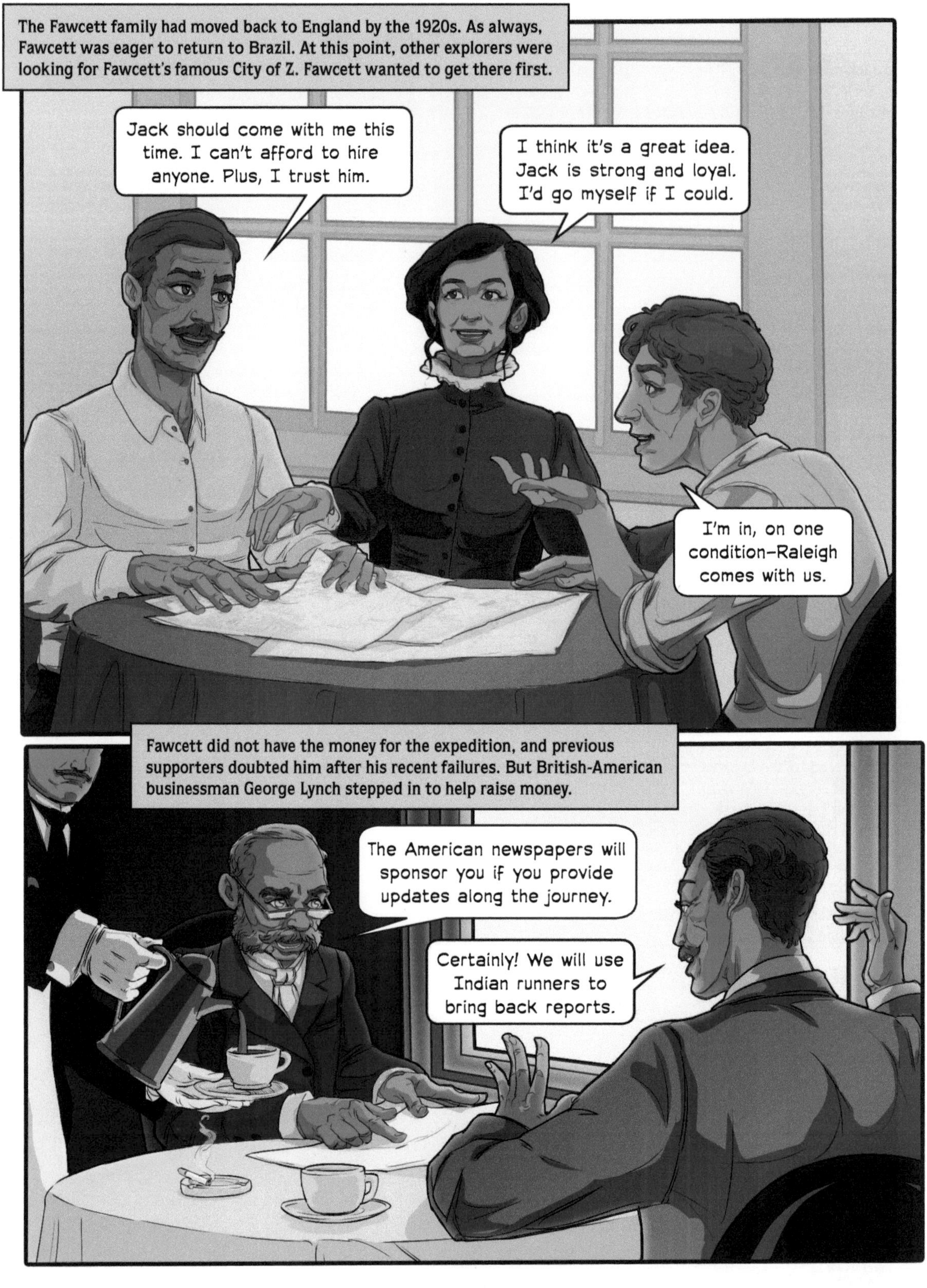
The Fawcett family had moved back to England by the 1920s. As always, Fawcett was eager to return to Brazil. At this point, other explorers were looking for Fawcett's famous City of Z. Fawcett wanted to get there first.
Jack should come with me this time. I can't afford to hire anyone. Plus, I trust him.
I think it's a great idea. Jack is strong and loyal. I'd go myself if I could.
I'm in, on one condition–Raleigh comes with us.
Fawcett did not have the money for the expedition, and previous supporters doubted him after his recent failures. But British-American businessman George Lynch stepped in to help raise money.
The American newspapers will sponsor you if you provide updates along the journey.
Certainly! We will use Indian runners to bring back reports.

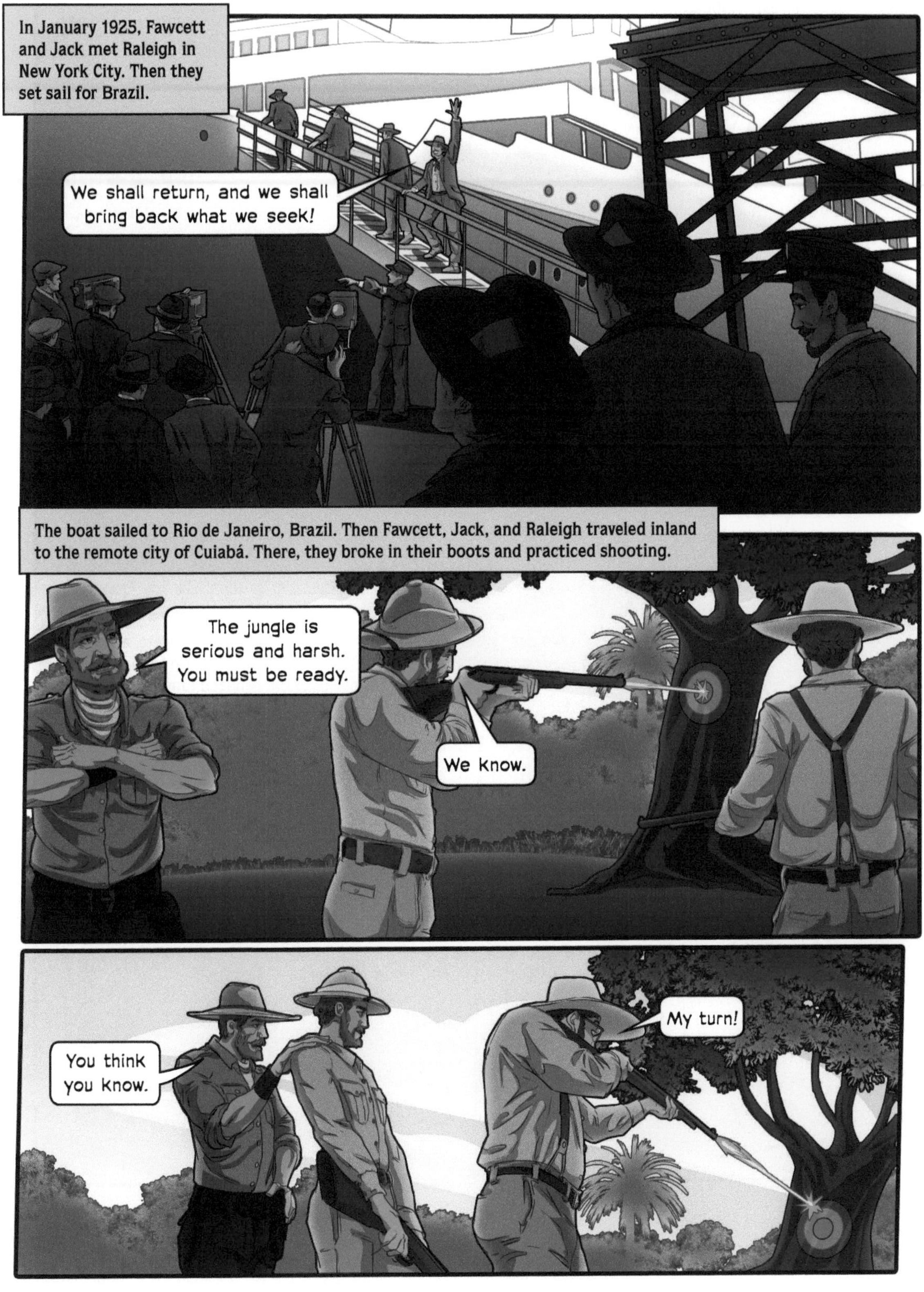
In January 1925, Fawcett and Jack met Raleigh in New York City. Then they set sail for Brazil.
We shall return, and we shall bring back what we seek!
The boat sailed to Rio de Janeiro, Brazil. Then Fawcett, Jack, and Raleigh traveled inland to the remote city of Cuiabá. There, they broke in their boots and practiced shooting.
The jungle is serious and harsh. You must be ready.
We know.
You think you know.
My turn!

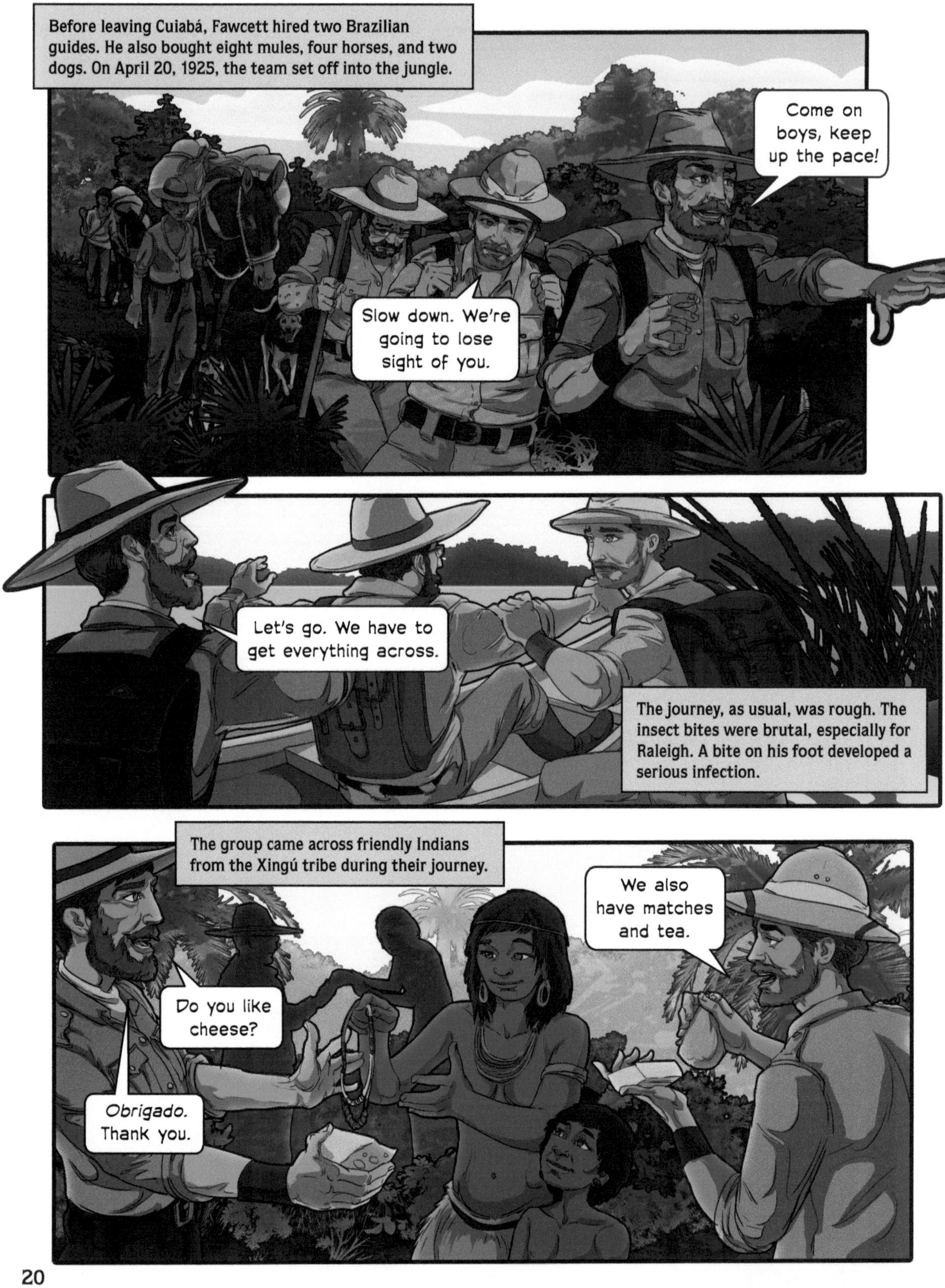
Before leaving Cuiabá, Fawcett hired two Brazilian guides. He also bought eight mules, four horses, and two dogs. On April 20, 1925, the team set off into the jungle.
Come on boys, keep up the pace!
Slow down. We're going to lose sight of you.
Let's go. We have to get everything across.
The journey, as usual, was rough. The insect bites were brutal, especially for Raleigh. A bite on his foot developed a serious infection.
The group came across friendly Indians from the Xingú tribe during their journey.
We also have matches and tea.
Do you like cheese?
Obrigado. Thank you.

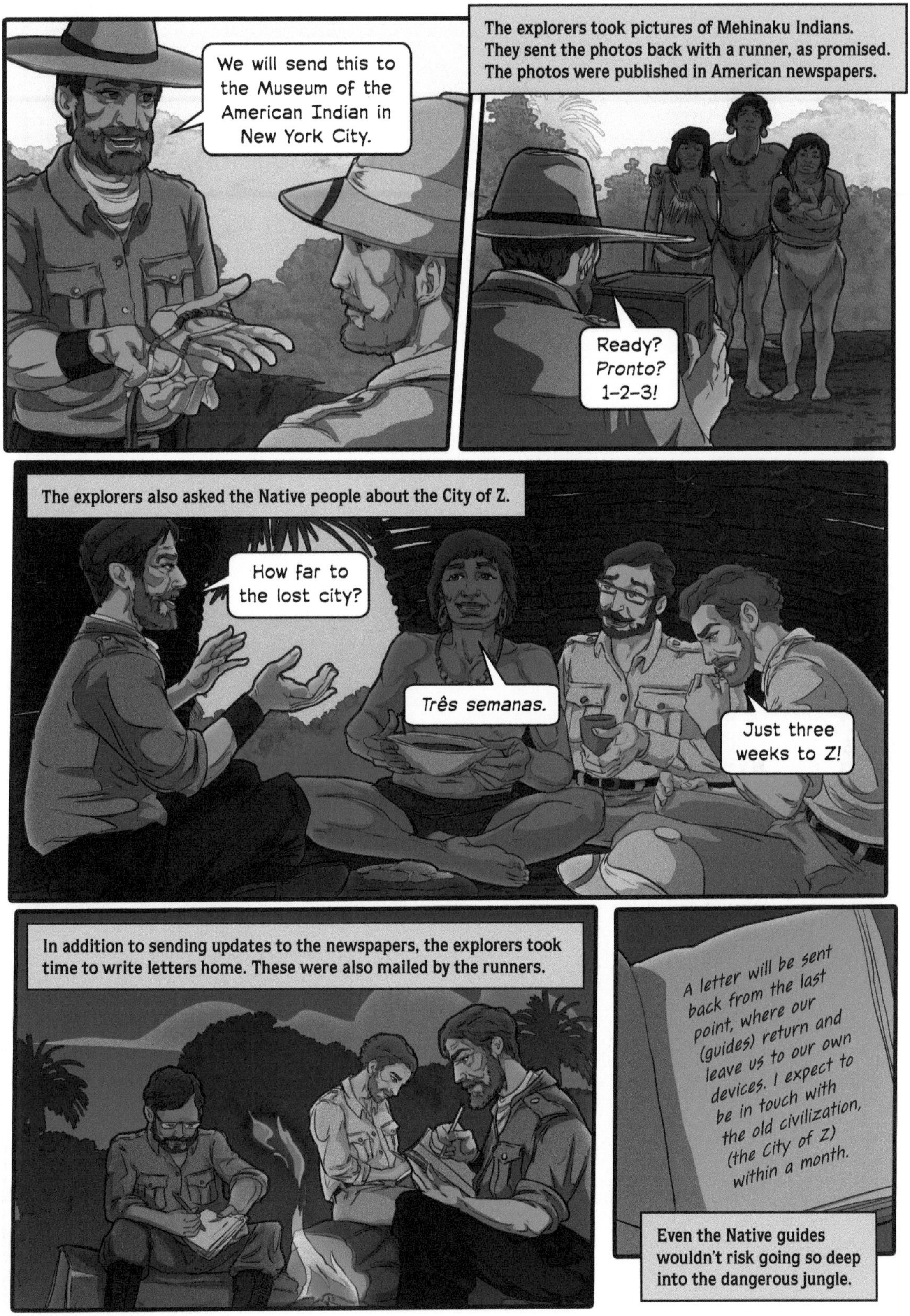
We will send this to the Museum of the American Indian in New York City.
The explorers took pictures of Mehinaku Indians. They sent the photos back with a runner, as promised. The photos were published in American newspapers.
Ready? *Pronto?* 1-2-3!
The explorers also asked the Native people about the City of Z.
How far to the lost city?
Três semanas.
Just three weeks to Z!
In addition to sending updates to the newspapers, the explorers took time to write letters home. These were also mailed by the runners.
A letter will be sent back from the last point, where our (guides) return and leave us to our own devices. I expect to be in touch with the old civilization, (the City of Z) within a month.
Even the Native guides wouldn't risk going so deep into the dangerous jungle.

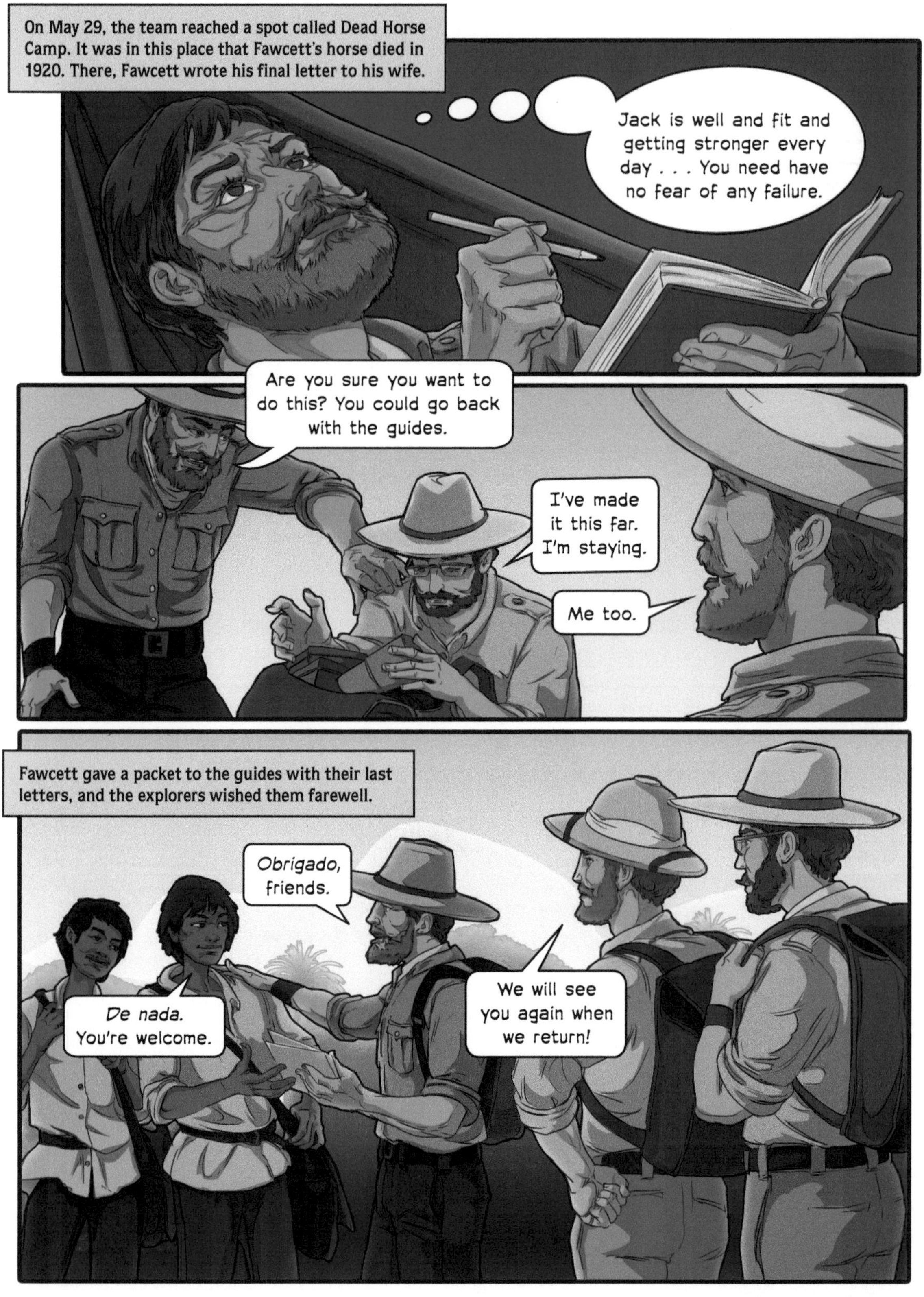
On May 29, the team reached a spot called Dead Horse Camp. It was in this place that Fawcett's horse died in 1920. There, Fawcett wrote his final letter to his wife.
Jack is well and fit and getting stronger every day . . . You need have no fear of any failure.
Are you sure you want to do this? You could go back with the guides.
I've made it this far. I'm staying.
Me too.
Fawcett gave a packet to the guides with their last letters, and the explorers wished them farewell.
Obrigado, friends.
De nada. You're welcome.
We will see you again when we return!

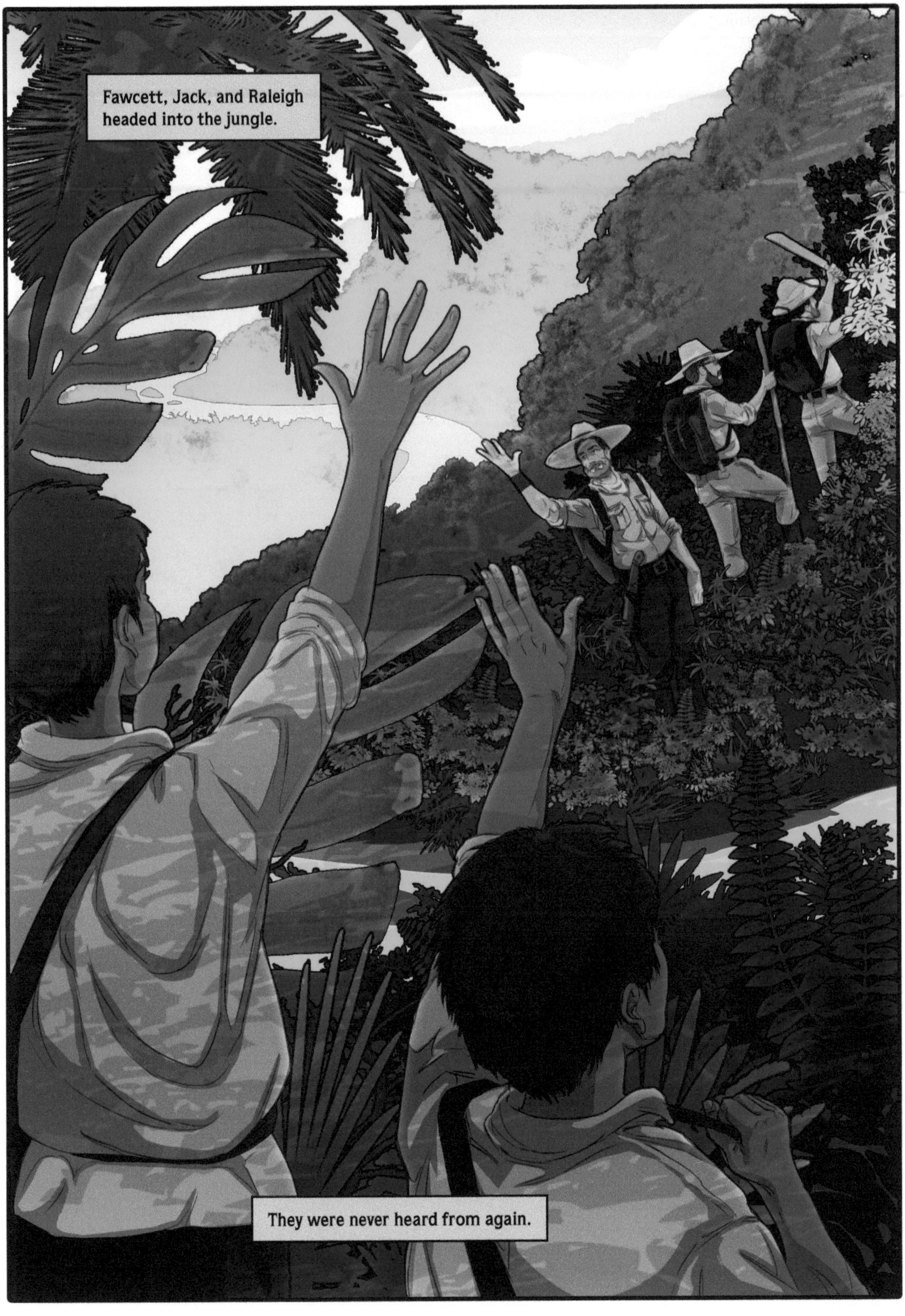
Fawcett, Jack, and Raleigh headed into the jungle.
They were never heard from again.

The Hunt for Fawcett

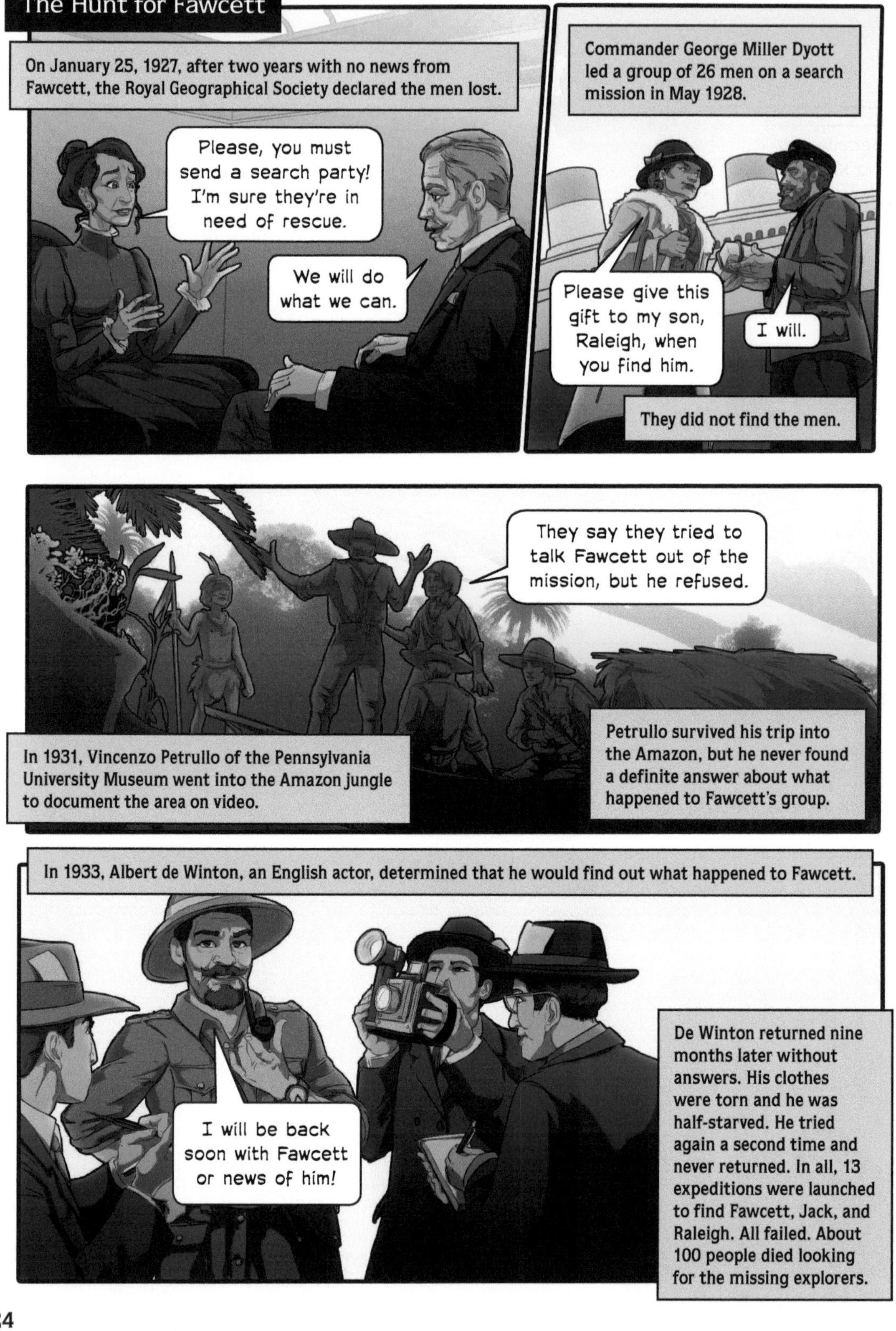
On January 25, 1927, after two years with no news from Fawcett, the Royal Geographical Society declared the men lost.
Please, you must send a search party! I'm sure they're in need of rescue.
We will do what we can.
Commander George Miller Dyott led a group of 26 men on a search mission in May 1928.
Please give this gift to my son, Raleigh, when you find him.
I will.
They did not find the men.
They say they tried to talk Fawcett out of the mission, but he refused.
In 1931, Vincenzo Petrullo of the Pennsylvania University Museum went into the Amazon jungle to document the area on video.
Petrullo survived his trip into the Amazon, but he never found a definite answer about what happened to Fawcett's group.
In 1933, Albert de Winton, an English actor, determined that he would find out what happened to Fawcett.
I will be back soon with Fawcett or news of him!
De Winton returned nine months later without answers. His clothes were torn and he was half-starved. He tried again a second time and never returned. In all, 13 expeditions were launched to find Fawcett, Jack, and Raleigh. All failed. About 100 people died looking for the missing explorers.

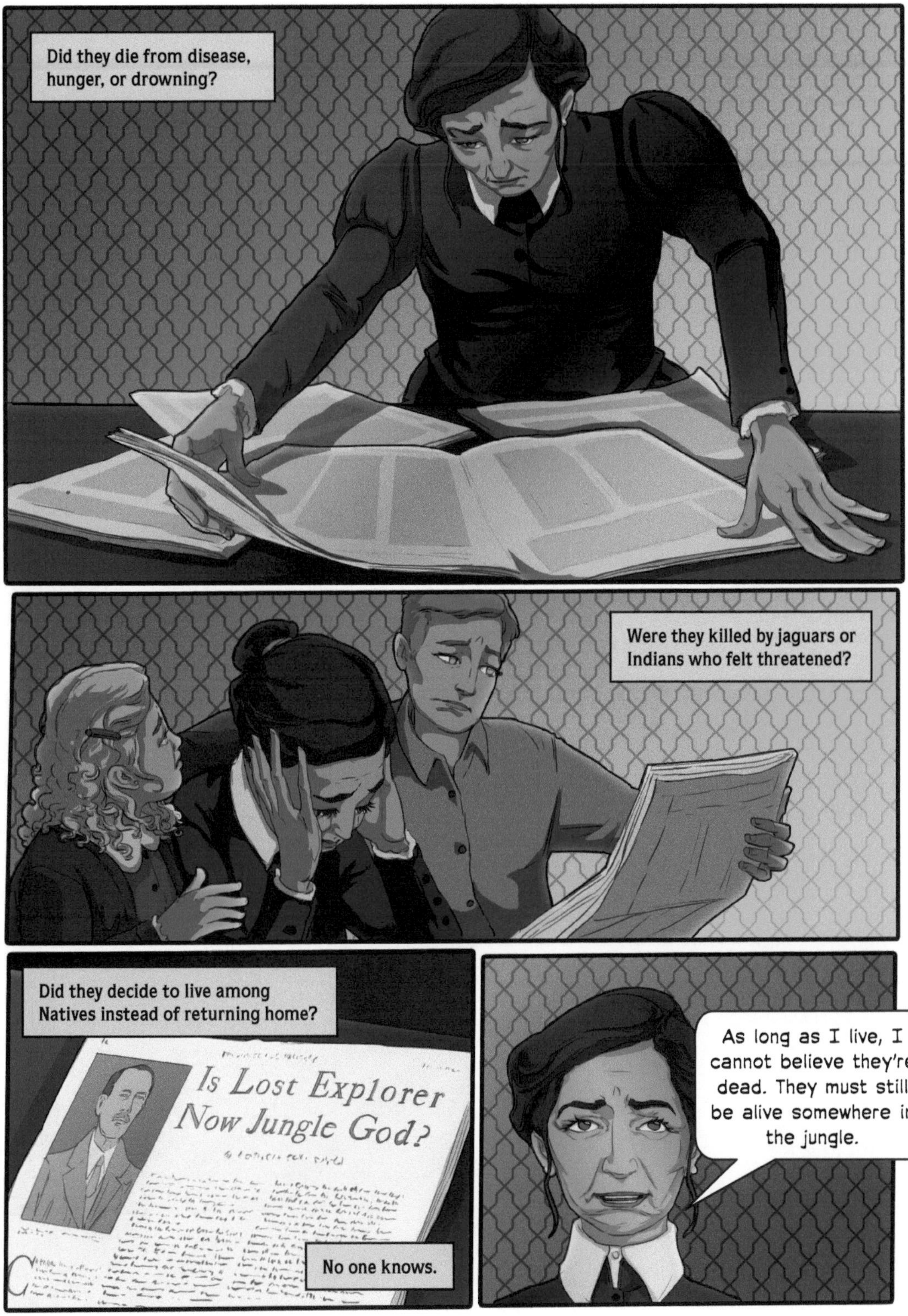
Did they die from disease, hunger, or drowning?
Were they killed by jaguars or Indians who felt threatened?
Did they decide to live among Natives instead of returning home?
Is Lost Explorer Now Jungle God?
No one knows.
As long as I live, I cannot believe they're dead. They must still be alive somewhere in the jungle.

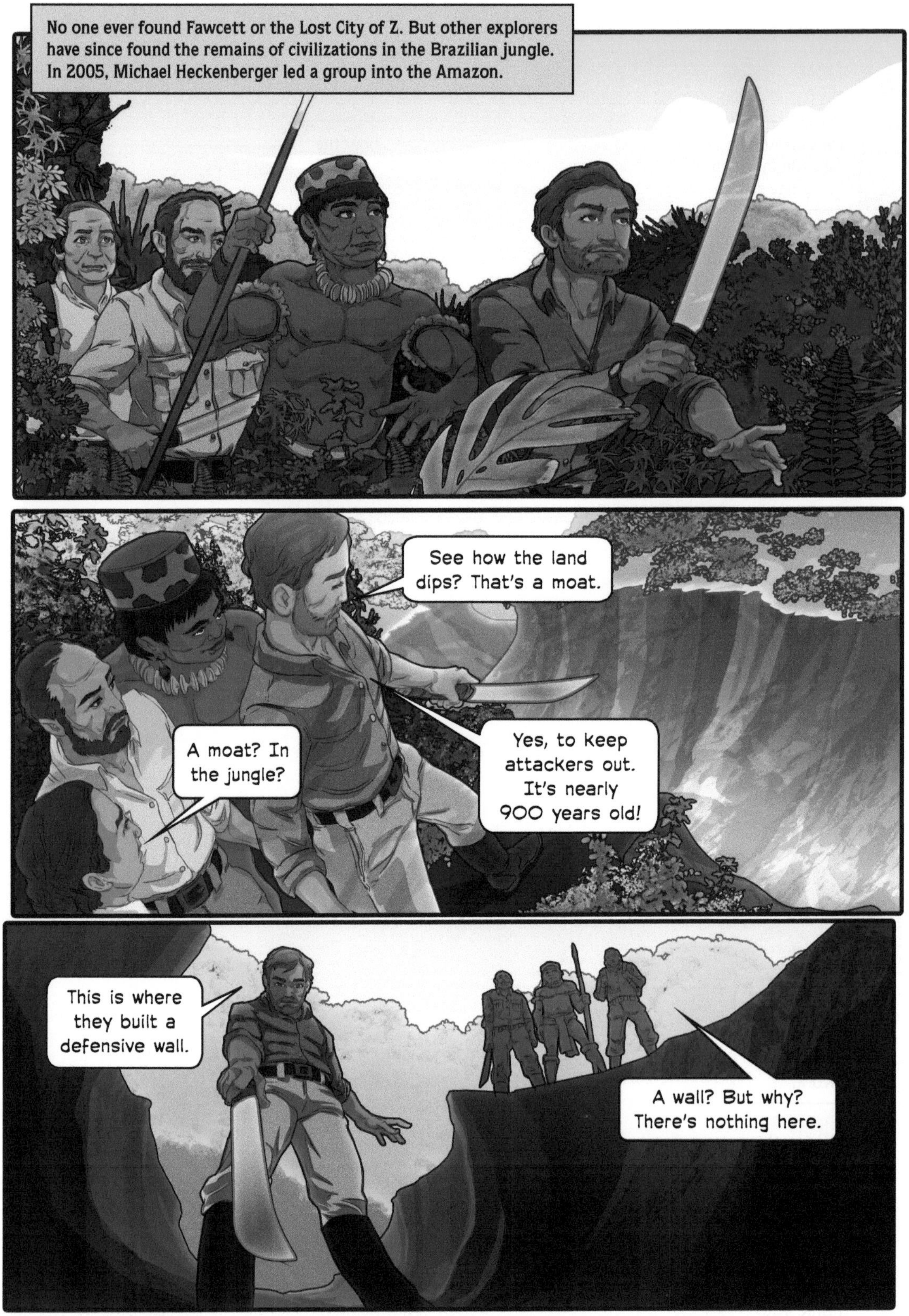
No one ever found Fawcett or the Lost City of Z. But other explorers have since found the remains of civilizations in the Brazilian jungle. In 2005, Michael Heckenberger led a group into the Amazon.
See how the land dips? That's a moat.
A moat? In the jungle?
Yes, to keep attackers out. It's nearly 900 years old!
This is where they built a defensive wall.
A wall? But why? There's nothing here.

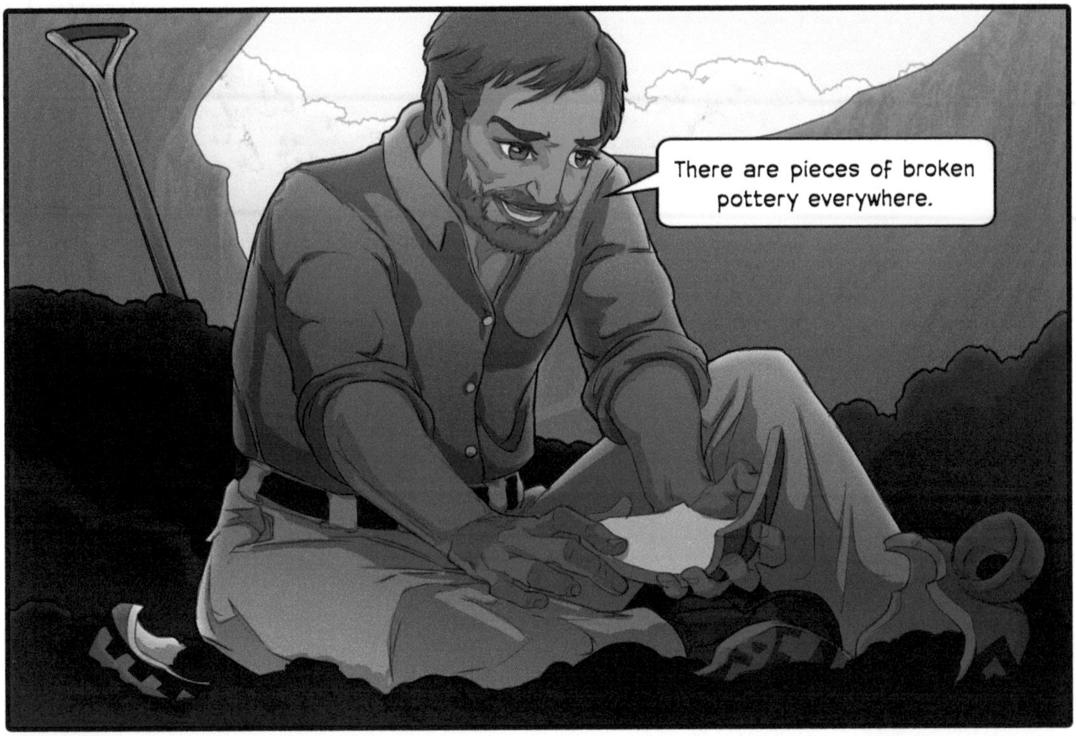
There are pieces of broken pottery everywhere.

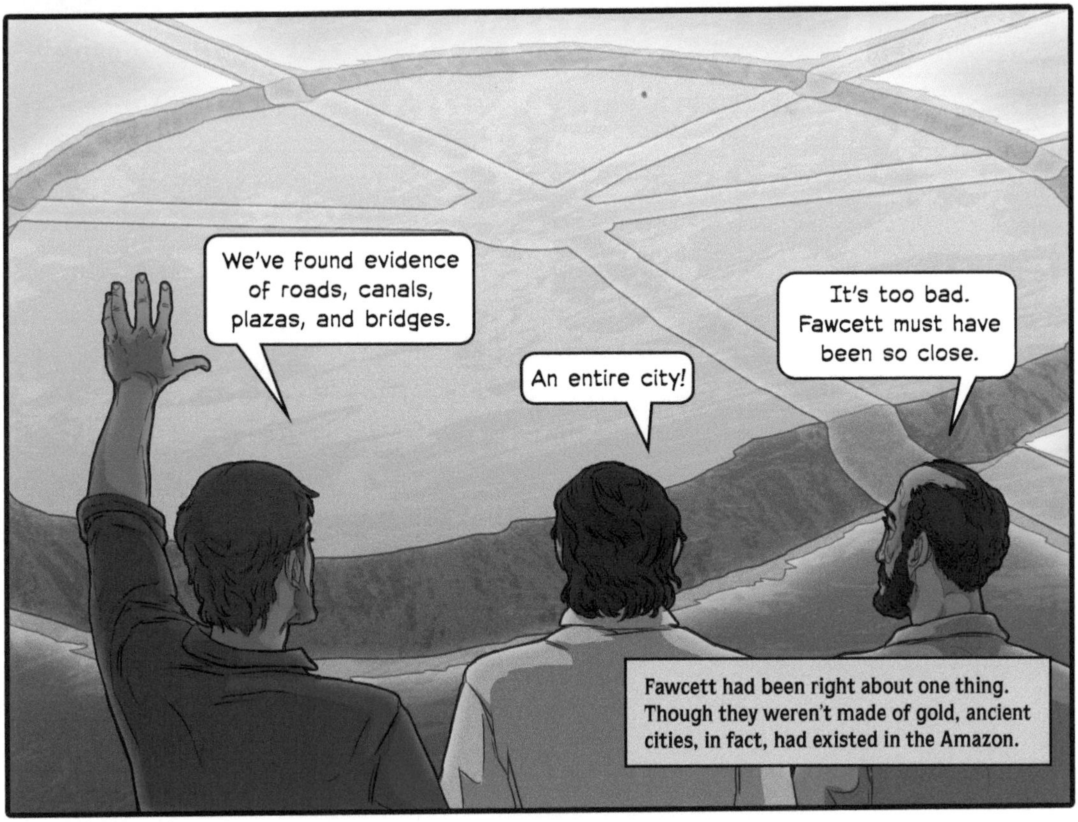
We've found evidence of roads, canals, plazas, and bridges.
An entire city!
It's too bad. Fawcett must have been so close.
Fawcett had been right about one thing. Though they weren't made of gold, ancient cities, in fact, had existed in the Amazon.

MAP OF THE EXPEDITION

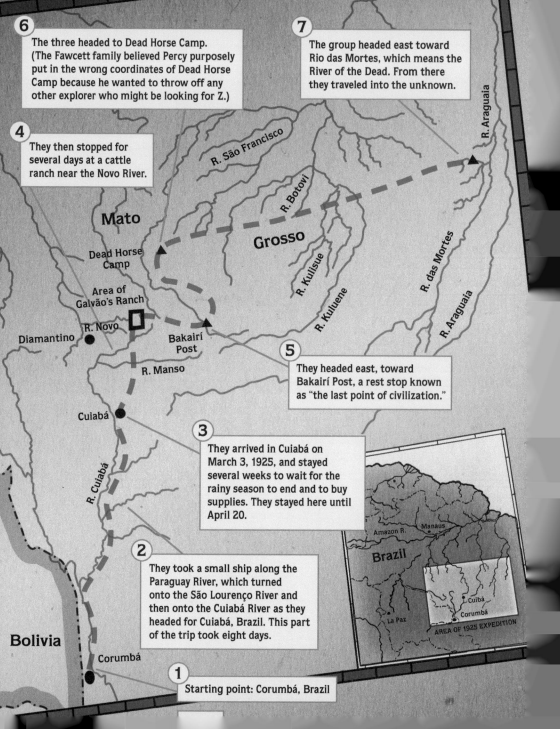

6 The three headed to Dead Horse Camp. (The Fawcett family believed Percy purposely put in the wrong coordinates of Dead Horse Camp because he wanted to throw off any other explorer who might be looking for Z.)

7 The group headed east toward Rio das Mortes, which means the River of the Dead. From there they traveled into the unknown.

4 They then stopped for several days at a cattle ranch near the Novo River.

R. São Francisco

R. Botovi

Mato

Grosso

Dead Horse Camp

R. Kulisue

R. das Mortes

Area of Galvão's Ranch

R. Novo

R. Kuluene

R. Araguaia

Diamantino

Bakairí Post

R. Manso

5 They headed east, toward Bakairí Post, a rest stop known as "the last point of civilization."

Cuiabá

3 They arrived in Cuiabá on March 3, 1925, and stayed several weeks to wait for the rainy season to end and to buy supplies. They stayed here until April 20.

R. Cuiabá

Amazon R.   Manaus

Brazil

2 They took a small ship along the Paraguay River, which turned onto the São Lourenço River and then onto the Cuiabá River as they headed for Cuiabá, Brazil. This part of the trip took eight days.

La Paz

Cuibá

Corumbá

AREA OF 1925 EXPEDITION

Bolivia

Corumbá

1 Starting point: Corumbá, Brazil

MORE ABOUT THE EXPEDITION

Percy Fawcett actually left behind instructions saying that if he did not return, no rescue parties should be sent. The trip was too dangerous.

By 1934, a dozen expeditions had gone into the jungle on Fawcett's trail. Several of them hadn't come back. Brazilian officials banned people from making the attempt. That did not stop others from trying, though.

In 1951, a Brazilian Indian rights activist, Orlando Villas Bôas, came out of the jungle with a skeleton he said was Fawcett's. An expert in London examined the bones and said they did not belong to Fawcett.

Many say Percy Fawcett was an inspiration for both the character Indiana Jones and Sir Arthur Conan Doyle's *The Lost World*.

GLOSSARY

accordion (uh-KOR-dee-uhn)—a musical instrument that players squeeze to make sound; accordions have keys and buttons

ancient (AYN-shunt)—from a long time ago

artifact (AR-tuh-fakt)—an object used in the past that was made by people

artillery (ar-TIL-uh-ree)—cannons and other large guns used during battles

evidence (EV-uh-duhnss)—information, items, and facts that help prove something to be true or false

expedition (ek-spuh-DI-shuhn)—a journey made for a particular reason

folklore (FOKE-lohr)—tales, sayings, and customs among a group of people

geographical (jee-uh-GRAF-i-kuhl)—relating to the study of Earth's surface, and its land and water features

mirage (muh-RAZH)—something that appears to be there but is not; mirages are caused by light rays bending where air layers of different temperatures meet

mission (MISH-uhn)—a planned job or task

Native (NAY-tuhv)—a person who originally lived in a place

sponsor (SPON-sur)—financial support of an event or project, usually in return for public acknowledgment

survey (SUHR-vay)—to measure land in order to make a map and possibly a plan for how to use it

tribe (TRIBE)—a group of people who share the same language and way of life

READ MORE

Loh-Hagan, Virginia. *The Search for El Dorado*. Ann Arbor, MI: Cherry Lake Publishing, 2021.

Mavrikis, Peter. *Christopher Columbus and the Americas: Separating Fact from Fiction*. North Mankato, MN: Capstone, 2022.

Noll, Elizabeth. *Machu Picchu*. Minneapolis: Bellwether Media, Inc., 2021.

INTERNET SITES

Brazil: Timeline and History Overview
ducksters.com/geography/country/brazil_history_timeline.php

The Enduring Mystery Behind Percy Fawcett's Disappearance
history.com/news/explorer-percy-fawcett-disappears-in-the-amazon

Lost Cities of the Amazon Revealed
nbcnews.com/id/wbna3077413

INDEX

AUTHOR BIO

Cindy L. Rodriguez is the author of the YA novel *When Reason Breaks* and has contributed to the anthology *Life Inside My Mind: 31 Authors Share Their Personal Struggles*. She has also written the text for *Volleyball Ace*, *Drill Team Determination*, and *Gymnastics Payback*, all part of the Jake Maddox series. Before becoming a teacher, she was an award-winning reporter for *The Hartford Courant* and researcher for *The Boston Globe*'s Spotlight Team. She is a founder of Latinxs in Kid Lit, a blog that celebrates children's literature by/for/about Latinxs. Cindy is a big fan of the three Cs: coffee, chocolate, and coconut. She is currently a middle school reading specialist in Connecticut, where she lives with her family.

ILLUSTRATOR BIO

Martin Bustamante is an illustrator and painter from Argentina. At the age of three, he was able to draw a horse "starting by the tail" as his mother always says. As a teenager, he found in movies like *Star Wars* and in books such as *Prince Valiant* by Hal Foster new and fascinating worlds full of colors, shapes, and atmospheres that became his inspiration for drawing. At that moment, drawing and painting became his passions. He started working as a professional illustrator and has worked for several editorials and magazines from Argentina, USA, and Europe.